THE FOOD AND COOKING OF
SHANGHAI
AND EAST CHINA

THE FOOD AND COOKING OF
SHANGHAI
AND EAST CHINA

75 regional recipes from Shanghai, Zhejiang, Fujian, Anhui, Jiangsu and Jiangxi

Terry Tan

This edition is published by Aquamarine, an imprint of Anness Publishing Ltd, Blaby Road, Wigston, Leicestershire LE18 4SE

info@anness.com

www.aquamarinebooks.com;
www.annesspublishing.com

If you like the images in this book and would like to investigate using them for publishing, promotions or advertising, please visit our website www.practicalpictures.com for more information.

Publisher: Joanna Lorenz
Project Editor: Kate Eddison
Text Editors: Jan Cutler and Catherine Best
Photography: Martin Brigdale
Food Stylist: Katie Giovanni
Prop Stylist: Martin Brigdale
Designer: Simon Daley
Illustrator: Rob Highton
Production Controller: Steve Lang

© Anness Publishing Ltd 2012

A CIP catalogue record for this book is available from the British Library.

Publisher's Note

Although the advice and information in this book are believed to be accurate and true at the time of going to press, neither the authors nor the publisher can accept any legal responsibility or liability for any errors or omissions that may have been made nor for any inaccuracies nor for any loss, harm or injury that comes about from following instructions or advice in this book.

Notes

• Bracketed terms are intended for American readers.

• For all recipes, quantities are given in both metric and imperial measures and, where appropriate, in standard cups and spoons. Follow one set of measures, but not a mixture, because they are not interchangeable.

• Standard spoon and cup measures are level. 1 tsp = 5ml, 1 tbsp = 15ml, 1 cup = 250ml/8fl oz.

• Australian standard tablespoons are 20ml. Australian readers should use 3 tsp in place of 1 tbsp for measuring small quantities.

• American pints are 16fl oz/2 cups. American readers should use 20fl oz/2.5 cups in place of 1 pint when measuring liquids.

• Electric oven temperatures in this book are for conventional ovens. When using a fan oven, the temperature will probably need to be reduced by about 10–20°C/20–40°F. Since ovens vary, check with your manufacturer's instruction book for guidance.

• The nutritional analysis given for each recipe is calculated per portion (i.e. serving or item), unless otherwise stated. If the recipe gives a range, such as Serves 4–6, then the nutritional analysis will be for the smaller portion size, i.e. 6 servings. The analysis does not include optional ingredients, such as salt added to taste.

• Medium (US large) eggs are used unless otherwise stated in the text.

Front cover shows Stir-fried Prawns and Ginkgo Nuts – for recipe see page 58.

Contents

Geography and climate

Eastern China comprises the huge metropolis of Shanghai, and the surrounding provinces of Jiangsu, Anhui, Zhejiang, Fujian and Jiangxi. The most notable feature of the region is the Yangtze River Delta, and water is the predominant element of the landscape. This area is largely low-lying, with ancient irrigated rice fields traversed by a vast network of canals, many of which date back centuries. Jiangsu, Shanghai, Fujian and Zhejiang all share a coastal position, meaning that the sea also plays a huge part in these lands.

South of the Yangtze

The Yangtze River Delta, also known as the Chang Jiang Delta, or the Golden Triangle of the Yangtze, generally comprises the triangular-shaped territory of Shanghai, southern Jiangsu Province and northern Zhejiang Province. The area lies at the heart of the region traditionally called Jiangnan (literally, 'south of the Yangtze River'). The Yangtze River is China's longest waterway, running over 6,300km

Right **With its long coastline and lush river delta green with paddy fields, eastern China is famous for its rice and fish dishes.**
Below **The eastern provinces share no international land borders, but do have a long coastal border to the east.**

(nearly 4,000 miles) on its epic journey from the Tibetan Plateau, past the Sichuan basin, then through the deep Yangtze gorges and the basins of Hubei and Anhui before it drains into the East China Sea. A vast network of lakes and tributaries slows down its progress as it winds its way through Jiangsu Province. Most of this vast river is navigable, and trade routes have

existed for many centuries between the different provinces of China along the river.

Not surprisingly, the cuisine of eastern China makes a clear distinction between the flavours of ocean fish and river fish, and freshwater fishing is extremely important. In Qingpu, 50 ponds containing five different species of fish yield 29,000 tons of fish each year.

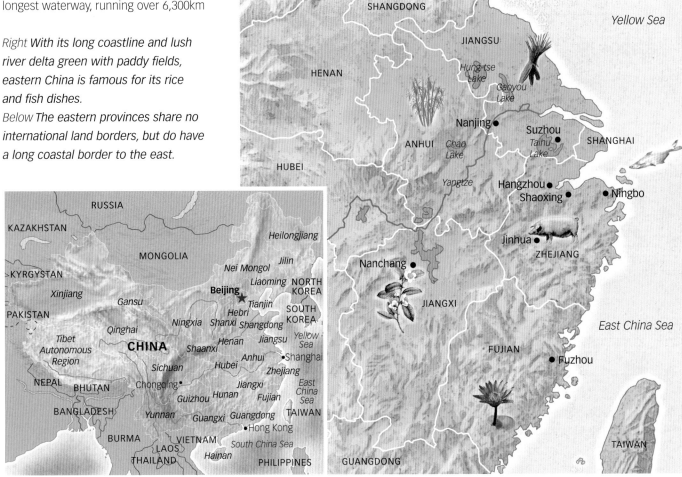

Left Tea plantations cling to the verdant hillsides of Zhejiang.

Above Traditional boats are still used to navigate the lakes of Jiangsu.

Climate and farming

Eastern China has a marine monsoon sub-tropical climate, and the weather is generally warm and humid. However, winter temperatures can drop as low as -10°C/14°F and, even in springtime, large temperature fluctuations can occur. The Yangtze River Delta contains the most fertile soils in all of China. Rice is the dominant crop of the delta, but further inland, fishing rivals it for supremacy. The other major crops of this region are tea and silk, both of which have been farmed here for hundreds of years.

Eastern provinces

Jiangsu is probably the most blessed province in eastern China, with lush wetlands and fertile land that supports abundant agriculture. It has been dubbed 'the land of fish and rice' ever since its ancient beginnings. This small area of China, only about 5 per cent of the land mass, provides about 40 per cent of China's wealth. This wealth comes mainly from the waterways of the mighty Yangtze and the stupendous Grand Canal

that slices its way from the north into the lower reaches of the lower delta region. Jiangsu is hot and humid in summer with cold, misty winters and plenty of rain – an ideal climate for growing rice.

Fujian's topography is dominated by soaring mountains, river valleys and a verdant sub-tropical coastline. The coastal ports have been magnets for international trade for centuries, but the forbidding, mountainous inland areas of this province were relatively inaccessible until the 1960s, when roads were built through the thick jungle. Sea fishing has been the main livelihood of Fujian's inhabitants for centuries.

Zhejiang is one of China's smallest provinces and is divided into two distinct areas. The flatter delta area north of Hangzhou, the capital of Zhejiang, is a verdant region of rolling hills, tea plantations and meandering rivers; the mountainous area to the south where it joins Fujian province is far less suited to agriculture. The benefits of this terrain are that southern Zhejiang offers much unspoilt beauty, with rugged mountains,

lofty peaks and expansive valleys. Hangzhou's tea plantations yield one of the world's most sensuous teas, Dragon Well Tea (Long Qing Cha). Near Hangzhou is the waterside city of Shaoxing, famous for its eponymous wine (often spelt Xiaoxing). While this wine may be imperfect by Western wine standards, it is nonetheless much loved by locals for its robust flavour. It is also ideal for cooking.

Urban development

The urban centres of eastern China are the major cities of Shanghai, Nanjing, Hangzhou, Suzhou and Ningpo. These share much the same climate – cold winters, contrasted with summers that often reach highs of a searing 40°C (over 100°F) with humidity to match. In modern times the area has developed tremendously fast, and has become known as the Yangtze Delta Metropolitan Area, the largest built-up area in China, covering 99,600sq km (38,500 square miles). It is home to over 90 million residents, of whom an estimated 50 million are part of the urban population.

History

Eastern China has a long history of farming, fishing and trade. This is a fertile region, suited to agriculture, and the population is correspondingly large and relatively prosperous. From the time of the Han dynasty (206BC–AD220) onwards, the Yangtze River Delta has been an area of high productivity, with its own traditions of culture, food and farming. Today, Shanghai is one of the world's largest cities, buzzing with modern technology, architecture and transport, and an ever-expanding population.

Shanghai – small beginnings to big city

The biggest city and most important port in China's eastern region, Shanghai dates back to the 10th century. It is a municipality with provincial status (in other words, it is big enough to have its own local government). Located in the Yangtze valley, it was a small market town with only 12,000 families living there until 1127, when sudden migration and refugee movements swelled the population twentyfold to some 250,000 people.

By the 13th century, Shanghai and the surrounding area became one of China's richest regions, producing cotton, the backbone of Shanghai's economy until the early 19th century. By the time of the Ming Dynasty, between the 14th and 17th centuries, the first shoots of capitalism in East China appeared and were nurtured in this area. Shanghai continued to grow throughout the rest of the Qing Dynasty (1644–1911), and became a large financial centre that gave important support to both large-scale agriculture and smaller farming enterprises.

Shanghai reached an economic peak in the early 19th century. The Qing rulers of China were not well organized and had little government control, so provincial guilds, termed Native Place Associations, used their extensive networks to control the city and began to compete with each other. During the Opium War of 1840, British forces temporarily held Shanghai. The war ended with the 1842 Treaty of Nanking, which saw Shanghai opened for international trade. The Taiping Rebellion broke out in 1850 and devastated the countryside but left the foreign settlements untouched.

From this uneasy situation two cities emerged: a chaotic Chinese city and a Westernized city, inhabited mainly by Chinese who preferred the Western lifestyle. This Westernized part of Shanghai has always been seen as one of the world's most modern cities. New inventions such as trams were introduced, and Shanghai was turned into a huge metropolis. British and American businessmen made a great deal of money in trade and finance here, and Germany used Shanghai as a base for investing in China. Today the city vibrates with a lively ambience that draws thousands of visitors from all over the world.

Jiangxi – 21st-century backwater

When the Grand Canal was built in the 7th century, linking China's major waterways, the inland province of Jiangxi suddenly became an important transit point on the overland trade route from Guangdong. Tea growing and silver mining soon created a wealthy merchant

Left The Grand Canal, which stretches from Beijing to Hangzhou, here winds its way through Suzhou in Jiangsu Province.

Anhui – the quiet province

Probably the least known among China's eastern provinces, Anhui has seen little of the frantic development permeating the rest of urban China today. The borders were defined by the Qing government in the 17th century and have remained largely unchanged over the centuries, although its location, set between the warring factions of northern and southern China, has meant the province has seen more than its fair share of fighting and government changes. This inland province contains fertile agricultural land in the north, where it consists mainly of flat river plains, and a far more mountainous region in the south. The contrast is so marked that the province was divided into two at the founding of the People's Republic of China, but Anhui was merged into one again in 1952.

Below The traditional architecture in Hongcun village in Anhui follows ancient feng shui principles.

class. By the 19th century, many coastal ports in this region created competition and Jiangxi's role became less prominent. Traditional and ancient Chinese junks, which made up most of the river craft, slowly disappeared. The province had a rather dubious reputation of being an important Communist guerrilla base in the 20th century, but after many years, the Kuomintang drove the Communists out and on to their 'Long March' to Shaanxi.

Fujian – trading province

The coastal areas of Fujian had been part of the Chinese empire since the Qin Dynasty (221–207BC). From its early beginnings as a frontier region it grew into a major commercial centre with important ports for the maritime silk route. Other commodities traded were precious stones, textiles, porcelain and food products, which were magnets to Arab merchants and other traders. Missionaries also came to the area. When the Ming emperors forced restrictions in the 16th century that affected this maritime trade, Fujian people began to emigrate to Taiwan, Singapore,

the Philippines, Malaysia and Indonesia; Fujian cuisine still exists today in these countries. The capital city, Fouzhou, is now a flourishing, bustling boom town with incredible skyscrapers and endless construction projects. The historical port of Xiamen (Amoy) is said to have been the birthplace of soy sauce, an ingredient which now enjoys a global status.

Regional cooking

The vibrant and modern city of Shanghai, situated on the Yangtze estuary, has spread its culinary culture well into the eastern provinces of Jiangsu, Zhejiang and even further south into Fujian. It is a municipality with provincial status and much influence, and is blessed by being located in an extremely fertile lower valley of the Yangtze River. The immense river and long coastline mean that, unsurprisingly, the amazing diversity of eastern recipes includes many exquisite fish and shellfish dishes.

Flavours of the river delta

The delta region is an enormously prolific rice bowl, providing this basic food for the whole of China. Shanghai dishes tend to be richer and heavier than those of Beijing or Cantonese cuisine, but the emphasis is still on freshness, with pure and natural flavours. The Yangtze River puts fish and shellfish at the heart of the food culture, and locally caught shrimps, crab, wild duck and carp feature strongly.

Shanghai cuisine

The culinary style of Shanghai is elegant, with fragrant sauces. Some Chinese cooks are of the opinion that Shanghai does not have its own definitive cuisine, but adopts and adapts those from the surrounding provinces, so that the resulting marriage of styles and ingredients is a hybrid with Shanghai soul. Shanghai chefs can be heavy-handed with alcohol, resulting in many 'drunken' dishes. Almost every creature that flies, swims or crawls is fair game for this delicious sousing.

Salted meats and preserved vegetables are commonly used to enhance dishes, and sugar is used with abandon, especially in tandem with soy sauce. 'Red cooking' (Hong Shao) is a popular style of stewing meats and vegetables in an intoxicating blend of wine, preserved bean curd and soy sauce.

There are many well-known and almost legendary recipes from Shanghai, such as Beggar's Chicken, a whole chicken wrapped in lotus leaves, covered in clay and oven-baked. Lime-and-ginger-flavoured 'hundred year eggs' are another popular Shanghai creation. Some may draw the line at eating 'Stinky Tofu', but it remains a delicacy of this region. There are many more: Lion's Head Pork Balls, an exquisite treat of succulent minced pork in a rich wine sauce; Sweet-and-Sour Spare Ribs, so well known in the West; and Stir-fried Eels in Hoisin Sauce – all rich and delicious products of Shanghai cuisine.

Below left Fish is dried on bamboo trays in Fujian province.
Below Rice is transplanted to a flooded paddy in Anhui, to be used in dishes all over China when harvested.

Cuisine of the other eastern provinces

The eastern school of cooking has more distinct provincial styles than other parts of China, the most high-profile being that of the Huai Yang style, which has its centre in Yangzhou. This gave the world the famous Yangzhou Fried Rice that features in Chinese restaurants across the world.

Jiangxi and Zhejiang share a border, and they also share many culinary elements, creating a food sub-school called the Jiangzhe style, which has an emphasis on grand banquet dishes served at festivals.

Hangzhou, in Zhejiang province, is famed for its Dragon Well Tea, Xiaoxing for its eponymous wine and Jinhua or Kin Hua for its superb ham. Rice wine goes into many dishes, in a style similar to that of Beijing cooking. Indigenous vegetables such as Chinese kale and cabbage appear in numerous dishes, often pickled in brine. Soy-braised duck and goose are regional specialities. The use of seasoning is quite restrained, allowing the natural flavours of the fresh ingredients to shine through. For the richer and saltier meat dishes, honey and maltose are used to flavour pork, sliced ham and chicken.

Fujian – a fresh style

In Fujian, cooking tends to be on the light side with an emphasis on steaming. As Fujian borders Guangdong, many dishes reflect Cantonese elements. Fish, which is a predominant ingredient in this coastal region, is touched only lightly with ginger, sesame oil, soy sauce and pepper. The same restraint applies to meat and poultry dishes. The lotus plant grows profusely in ponds, lakes and streams in this area, and its leaves are used for wrapping many fillings. Lotus nuts are also used in cooking, while lotus blossom is revered in Taoism.

Anhui – unusual specialities

The cuisine of Anhui is perhaps the misfit of the eastern region, as it has many recipes containing rarer culinary ingredients such as frogs, turtles, pigeons, partridges and pangolins. Cooks also make lavish use of mushrooms, bayberries, tea leaves, bamboo shoots and dates, as well as game animals from the mountainous area of Huangshan. Here in the highlands, white and tender bamboo shoots grow in abundance and appear in dozens of dishes. Anhui chefs are particular about preserving the natural flavour of ingredients and tend to add seasonings very judiciously.

Above left Shaoxing wine, a fermented rice wine, is made in Zhejiang Province, then transported around the world to be used in many recipes.
Above Jinhua ham is a famous air-dried ham from Zhejiang, which is used in many stewed and braised dishes to give depth of flavour.
Below Dragon Well Tea, from Hangzhou in Zhejiang Province, is one of eastern China's favourite green teas. It is usually picked by hand and is famous for its high quality.

Festivals and customs

While the Gregorian calendar is followed for all practical purposes in China, it is the lunar calendar that governs the cultural, festive, religious and spiritual life of Chinese people. Most of the important celebrations, such as Lunar New Year and the Moon Cake Festival, have evolved over thousands of years and are intrinsic to life throughout China. However, there are some less well-known festivals, such as the Cold Food Festival described below, that are closely tied to local history and traditions.

Lunar New Year

Shanghai sees in the Lunar New Year with a veritable explosion of fireworks all over the city. Family and friends get together and indulge in Yangge dancing and lion dancing. The origins of the Yangge dance can be traced back 2,000 years to a religious activity to greet the gods and dispel evil. Today it is less allied with its religious past, and has become more of a party in this most outward-looking of Chinese cities. Fireworks have spiritual significance – they are meant to see out the old and bring in the new. Everyone in the family must wear new clothes on the morning of Lunar New Year's Day and the older population will visit temples, bringing offerings of food, wine and even live poultry to appease the gods.

Moon Cake Festival

There are many legends about this festival, but one in particular is singled out for its charm. A Taoist priest boasted that he could take his Tang emperor to the moon palace, then threw his walking stick into the sky. It turned into a bridge and they both went to the moon palace. They spent many joyous years on the moon and on their return the people celebrated by making round cakes to signify this lunar journey.

Another oddity of the eastern provinces is Moon Cake Gambling, a game invented by a former Fujian pirate-cum-patriot to keep his buccaneers from being homesick. Every mid-autumn festival, a game of dice is played in a large porcelain bowl to compete for moon cakes. Prizes range

*Below left **New Year decorations adorn a street in Shanghai**.*
*Below **A man makes a traditional sweet for Lunar New Year in Zhejiang Province**.*

from tiny cookies to large moon cakes, the different sizes representing the official positions won in the imperial examinations. While few people take this history seriously, they enjoy going through the motions of the game, though fruits, wine and other foods are often awarded as prizes, rather than moon cakes.

Tin Hau Festival

While predominantly celebrated in Guangdong and Hong Kong, this festival is also popular in Fujian Province due to its fishing heritage. Tin Hau, the Goddess of the Sea, is known here as the Queen of Heaven and the Mother of all fishermen, and was supposed to have been born in Fujian in 1093. There is an interesting story behind this holy figure: one day, as usual, her father and brothers went far out to sea to fish, but at home, Tin Hau had a dream that her father and brothers were drowning. She flew over the deep sea on clouds and rescued her family. It is also believed that Tin Hau predicted storms and told travellers' fortunes.

Ching Ming (Clear and Bright) Festival

One festival in particular is followed with great reverence in the eastern provinces. In death, as in life, Chinese people celebrate or commiserate with special foods. The Ching Ming Festival falls in early April and it is a day when families visit graveyards to pay respects to their ancestors, offer food to the God of the Earth and generally spend a day picnicking on the site. There is great reverence in these sombre festivities, for Taoism embraces ancestor worship and filial piety extends to the afterlife.

Cold Food Festival

This is an unusual celebration, hardly known outside Fujian. It has its origins in Taiwan, as most Taiwanese are of Fujian extraction. On 4 April each year, fire and smoke are taboo. According to legend, a court official from 2,000 years ago was burned to death on that day, and in remembrance, the Fujian Chinese used to forgo the use of fire for an entire month. This abstinence has now become just a single day, on which the residents of

Above A boy makes an offering at a family headstone during Ching Ming. Above left Children make moon cakes in school to learn about the ancient festival.

Fujian will eat only cold food, such as spring rolls and even cold noodles. Interestingly, these days some people regard the day as a quirky challenge and eat only cold cheeseburgers.

Eat Leizaisu

It is believed that the birthday of Leizun, an important personage of Suzhou, falls on 24 June. The festival of Eat Leizaisu dictates that everyone goes vegetarian for one day out of respect for Leizun. This is also believed to prevent disaster, avoid epidemic disease and ensure everlasting peace. In the past, the people of Suzhou celebrated this green festival for a whole month, generally in June, but nowadays they are more likely to celebrate it for just a few days. The end of the festival is marked with a special noodle dish known as Luya Noodles.

Tools and equipment

Chinese cooks have traditionally used certain pans and utensils, the shape and function of which has remained almost unchanged for centuries. Natural materials such as clay, metal and bamboo are still preferred to more modern inventions for cooking and serving food, and the most popular cooking methods rely on direct heat, such as stir-frying or steaming. The few modern inventions found in Chinese kitchens, such as electric rice cookers, tend to be new versions of the traditional tried and tested utensils.

The simplest items, particularly a round-based wok and a heavy, sharp cleaver, are ideal for all kinds of cooking and food preparation, and will be found in every Chinese kitchen. Bamboo, a revered plant in China, is used both as a woven steamer and in the form of chopsticks.

Woks and ladles
The wok dates back centuries to the time of nomadic tribes in North China. Since these people were always on the move with their animals, searching for the best grazing sites, they needed a utensil with a rounded base that could rest on a few rocks over a makeshift fire. The wok was born and has never changed its basic shape since then. They are now popular around the world for cooking Chinese dishes. The wok does multiple duty in most Chinese households, acting as a steamer, a braising pan, a frying pan and even a shallow boiler.

Electric woks are a recent innovation but are not perfect, as the heat is moderate and they do not reach the high temperatures needed for quick stir-frying. However, electric woks are ideal for slow braising and steaming. Cast iron – an alloy of iron and carbon – is still the best material for woks, although cast aluminium, being much lighter and less expensive, is increasingly used.

The traditional wok ladle is shaped at an angle that corresponds to the curvature of the wok for better scooping and more efficient stir-frying, as the blade has a broader area than a wooden spoon and other conventional ladles.

Cleaver
This unique Chinese knife is made from tempered iron or steel, honed to razor sharpness. The best size is about 30cm/12in in length and 10cm/4in wide, with a wooden handle, although these days they are often made of one whole piece of metal. The cleaver provides essential leverage for cutting through bone and large pieces of meat, and is a versatile implement – it can be used as a carver, crusher, slicer and chopper. The blunt end serves as a makeshift mallet for tenderizing meats.

Left Woks can be used for deep-frying as well as many other kinds of cooking. A wire skimmer is useful for removing cooked ingredients from the oil.

Above **Traditional steamers are made from bamboo, but they can be created using all sorts of materials today.**

Above **Chopsticks are the essential Chinese tool for eating most foods, and can also be used as a cooking utensil.**

Above **A rice cooker can be a useful investment for households where a lot of Chinese food is enjoyed.**

Clay or sand pot

This Chinese dish comes with a single handle and serves as an oven-to-table utensil when food is to be served piping hot or sizzling. Traditional clay pots have a wire frame to support the structure as the intense heat can cause cracks. This kind of pot is never used for the whole cooking process. Dishes are cooked in a wok or other utensil and then transferred to the clay pot, which is pre-heated just enough to maintain the temperature at the table.

Steamer

These are traditionally made of woven bamboo, but they may also be made of aluminium, with multiple perforated trays to allow the steam to come through each layer. Steamers come in many sizes, small enough to contain bite-sized morsels (as in dim sum) or large enough to contain several chickens. Multiple stack steamers are ideal for cooking several dishes at the same time.

Steamboat

This kind of cooking pot originated in Mongolia, in the far north of the country. They are sometimes called fire pots or hot pots, and are usually made of brass-coated or enamel-coated metal with a funnel in the centre of a moat that contains stock or water. The whole dish used to be heated over charcoal, although it is common these days to see electric models with thermostatic controls. Various foods are cut up and placed around the steamboat so that diners can cook the food themselves in the stock, using brass wire spoons.

Bamboo draining baskets

Ubiquitous in all South-east Asian countries, these versatile utensils are used for a multitude of purposes – as sieves (strainers), for draining soaked rice or even as food covers that allow air circulation and keep out flying insects. They are, in fact, simply the Chinese version of a colander.

Chopsticks

For many centuries, the Chinese have used chopsticks made from bamboo as they have a slightly rough texture, which is best for picking up slippery foods such as noodles and sauce-based dishes. Normal chopsticks are 22cm/9in long, but longer ones – up to twice this length – are used for turning deep-fried foods, keeping the user at a safe distance from spitting hot oil.

Rice cookers

These are ubiquitous in Chinese homes, and are no longer regarded as a novelty in the West, as many restaurants have made use of this marvellous Japanese invention. Electric models now also have clever features for keeping rice warm for up to an hour. They work on the principle of weight – when all the liquid is absorbed or evaporates, the inner container, which sits on a spring-loaded element, rises automatically, switching the appliance off.

Classic ingredients

Shanghai and the neighbouring provinces all boast their own unique cuisines, which make excellent use of the local produce. Together, they are intrinsically linked by the use of ingredients from their shared environment: the abundant fresh fish and shellfish from the sea, river and lakes; the rice grown in the lush Yangtze delta area; the local alcohols, which are are utilized in a plethora of recipes; the fabulous array of fresh fruits and vegetables; and the high-quality meat and poultry from local farms.

The cuisine of Shanghai is famous for its elegant flavour combinations and rich, fragrant dishes. It takes inspiration from all the surrounding provinces and incorporates their tastes and techniques into its own cuisine. All of the eastern regions have their own culinary identities, but what unites them is a love and appreciation of the fresh ingredients that are produced locally.

Rice

The lush Yangtze river delta provides an ideal environment for growing endless fields of rice, which means it

Below, left to right Glutinous rice, jasmine rice and rice wine vinegar.

forms part of almost every meal in these eastern Chinese provinces. Rice tends to be boiled or steamed and then, when cooked, can form the basis of fried rice dishes, such as the iconic Yangzhou Fried Rice. Rice porridge or congee is the most popular rice dish in Fujian-style meals and uses either short grain or broken rice to achieve the smooth consistency that is much loved by the community. The rice is cooked until it resembles oat porridge or Italian risotto, with a lot of milky liquid remaining.

Glutinous rice Also known as sticky rice, glutinous rice has a firm but sticky texture, which makes it perfect for stuffed rice dishes.

Jasmine rice This is very popular in eastern China, with its subtly delicate scent and dry, thin and firm grains that are translucent when raw.

Rice flour Used to make cakes such as Pumpkin Cake (the New Year favourite from Fujian), rice flour is also used as a thickener for stews.

Rice wine This is widely used in the cooking of eastern China, and the area is famous for its array of 'drunken' dishes. Zhejiang is the provincial home of the famous Shaoxing rice wine, and here and throughout the rest of eastern China it is used in copious amounts.

Rice vinegar Clear and clean-tasting, rice vinegar is widely used in Fujian cuisine due to its lovely aroma and subtle acidity.

Noodles

Although not as important as rice in Shanghai cuisine, noodles are ideal for making a complete dish, and can be eaten at any time of day. Usually made of wheat or rice flour, they can be thick or thin, fresh or dried.

Fine rice noodles Also known as rice vermicelli, fine rice noodles are sold dried. A special Fujian type, mee sua, is extremely thin and delicate, and is often reserved for soup, such as the famous Shanghai dish Liver and Kidney in Fine Noodles, and for special occasions.

Wheat noodles These come in three types: dried, semi-dried or fresh. Dried noodles double in bulk when cooked, whereas fresh ones retain the same weight. Some wheat noodles also contain egg, and these are known as Shanghai-style noodles. They resemble Japanese udon noodles and are usually sold fresh.

Mung bean noodles These are also known as cellophane or glass noodles. They are sold dry but reconstitute quickly in water and keep their crunch no matter how long they are cooked for, making them a good addition to some soups.

Spices and flavourings

The cuisine of eastern China of full of strong and surprising tastes, often derived from a subtle combination of ingredients that have been used there for centuries.

Garlic This universal bulb is used as an aromatic in many stir-fries.

Ginger Root ginger is used ground, chopped or puréed in many dishes. Pickled ginger is common in eastern China as an accompaniment.

Black bean sauce Soya beans are roasted and fermented with salt, until black and pungent. They are left whole or ground into a thick paste.

Yellow bean sauce This salty sauce is actually brown in colour, and is made from fermented soya beans.

Chilli bean paste This ingredient originates in Sichuan, but is now used all over China. It is a purée of ground dried chillies and yellow bean paste.

Hoisin sauce This sweet sauce is made from yellow bean paste and sugar, and is dark mahogany in colour. It is famous for being served with crispy aromatic duck or Peking duck, but is also used in many eastern Chinese stews and red-cooked dishes.

Soy sauce This essential condiment, now popular all over the world, comes in light and dark varieties. Light soy sauce provides seasoning to most dishes. Dark soy sauce is used as a salting agent, as well as adding colour to stews and marinades.

Vinegar Black and red vinegars are essential souring agents in soups, and are also used in dips. They are usually made from rice.

Sesame oil This oil has a strong nutty taste and is usually used in small quantities to provide a top note in soups and stir-fries. It is never used for deep-frying.

Five-spice powder This mix of spices is extremely piquant, so a little goes a long way. There are a few variants of it (and it does not have to contain just five spices), but it is most commonly composed of ground star anise, cinnamon, cloves, Sichuan peppercorns and fennel seeds. It can be rubbed on to meats before they are cooked, such as in the recipe, Marinated Duck.

Below, left to right **Mee sua, ginger and black bean sauce.**

Above, left to right **Pork ribs, pomfret and tiger prawns (jumbo shrimp).**

Poultry, eggs and meat

Although beef and lamb do appear occasionally on the menus of eastern China, pork is the most popular meat of the area, along with chicken and duck. Some more unusual meats dot the menus too, particularly in Anhui.

Chicken One of the most widely eaten foods in China, chicken forms a large part of the eastern menu and can be cooked in a wide variety of ways. Chicken is thought to have many medicinal properties.

Duck As it is tougher than chicken, duck is confined to fewer dishes than chicken, and recipes tend to involve lengthy marinating and cooking times, giving wonderful results.

Eggs Hen's eggs, quail's eggs and duck eggs are all eaten in eastern China. Salted duck eggs are boiled and eaten with congee. They are made by steeping raw duck eggs in salted water for a few weeks, then they are boiled, which makes their whites turn opaque and their yolks a brilliant orange.

Pork This is the main meat used in eastern Chinese cooking. Belly pork must have the perfect ratio of meat, fat and skin. Pork ribs sold in Chinese stores are cut with a generous amount of meat. Pork chops are not common in eastern cuisine, but do appear occasionally.

Ham Jinhua ham, a dry-cured ham from Zhejiang, is used in many dishes.

Other meats Lamb and beef will star in the occasional dish, but are much rarer than pork on the local menus.

Offal Chinese cooks are very skilled at elevating offal to great culinary heights.

Fish and shellfish

The coastal waters off Jiangsu, Zhejiang and Fujian provinces are bursting with fish and shellfish, and inland rivers in the Yangtze Delta around Shanghai are extremely rich with freshwater fish.

Anchovies Best known in their dried form, anchovies are used as a seasoning agent, especially in soups.

Eels Highly prized, eels feature in stewed Shanghai dishes with lots of wine and vinegar, especially female eels, which tend to be larger than males. They are almost always sold alive as they spoil quickly.

Pomfret These fish come in two types: black or white. They range in size from 13cm/5in to 23cm/9in.

Red snapper These brightly coloured fish have a delicate flavour and are highly prized in eastern China.

Crab Several types of crab feature in Chinese cooking, the most common being the mottled or flower crab, named for the pale blue pattern on its shell.

Prawns (shrimp) Both marine and freshwater prawns are highly prized in China. They come in various shapes and sizes. The larger ones are usually cooked whole, whereas small ones are dried and then used as a flavouring.

Mussels These are simply steamed or cooked in Chinese wine with aromatics. Allow 450g/1lb per person.

Scallops Regarded as a sophisticated shellfish, scallops are often served simply steamed with ginger and garlic.

Squid Consumed all along the coast, squid is plentiful and popular in eastern China.

Fish balls Excess fish is processed into balls and cakes. They are generally boiled or steamed first, then fried. Shrimp balls can be made at home, using minced prawns (shrimp).

Vegetables

Although they are rarely eaten raw, vegetables form an important part of most meals throughout China, with the eastern provinces being no exception. Within Buddhist communities, vegetarian stews and stir-fries are common.

Aubergines (eggplants) The most common type of aubergine is long and thin, and a green or purple colour. Choose aubergines with smooth unblemished skin and firm flesh. It is a very versatile ingredient and can be cooked in myriad ways.

Bamboo shoots These pale yellow or creamy white shoots have a crunchy texture and a distinctive taste. Fresh shoots have to be boiled for at least half an hour before eating; canned shoots can be used immediately.

Beansprouts Ubiquitous throughout China, beansprouts can be eaten raw but are usually added to stir-fried noodles to give crunch. They are delicate and highly nutritious.

Chinese leaves (Chinese cabbage) Having a sweet, delicate aroma and crunchy texture, Chinese leaves are commonly used in stir-fries, stews, soups or salads.

Chinese spinach The flavour of Chinese spinach is more robust than ordinary spinach, and it has a firmer texture. If you can't find it, you can use ordinary spinach instead.

Pak choi (bok choy) This green vegetable is excellent in stir-fries and is widely available in Chinese stores.

Mustard greens These large, pale green vegetables have a sharp and robust flavour. When blanched, they become mellower in taste and lose some of their bitterness.

Mooli (daikon) This root vegetable looks like a large white carrot and is crisp, juicy and slightly spicy in flavour. It can be eaten raw or cooked.

Leeks Chinese cooks are very fond of leeks and often use them as an alternative to garlic.

Spring onions (scallions) These are used as a vegetable in their own right, as well as being used finely sliced as a garnish.

Coriander (cilantro) These leaves are indispensable as a garnish for soups and stews, either chopped or as whole leaves. They are sold fresh and only keep for a day or two.

Above, left to right Bamboo shoots, *beansprouts and shiitake mushrooms.*

Dried and preserved vegetables The warm climate of eastern China means that preserving vegetables for the winter is not as vital as it is in the north. Dried and preserved vegetables are mainly used for their concentrated flavour. They include lily buds or 'golden needles', preserved mustard greens, preserved winter vegetables, salted vegetables and dried cole.

Gourds and squashes Coming in a bewildering variety of shapes and sizes, gourds and squashes include bitter melon, fuzzy melon, luffa squash and winter melon.

Mushrooms There is a huge variety of mushrooms used in Shanghai and eastern Chinese cuisine, including shiitake, cloud ear (wood ear), enoki, oyster, silver ear and straw mushrooms.

Tubers, aquatic roots and seeds These unusual ingredients are used in many dishes in eastern China. Cassava, lotus roots and seeds, ginkgo nuts, jicama, taro (yam) and water chestnuts are all used to add flavour and bulk.

Above, left to right Fried tofu, red fermented tofu and pineapple.

Tofu

Not regarded as a meat substitute in China, tofu (also called beancurd) is revered by all Chinese people and is put to use in many dishes. It is valued for its nutritional properties, being rich in protein, low in calories and free from cholesterol. It is available in many forms.

Fresh tofu Blocks of white tofu are available in soft or firm varieties. The soft or 'silken' variety is best used in soups and steamed dishes, whereas the firm variety is best in stir-fries and as a filling, as it is more robust and less likely to break up in the wok.

Dried tofu These sticks of tofu must be soaked in water to rehydrate before they can be used. This will soften them.

Fried tofu This product is made by frying tofu until a brown skin forms, and it has many uses in Chinese cooking. You can fry it yourself, if you like, by cutting fresh tofu into 2.5cm/1in cubes and deep-frying them slowly, until golden. Fried tofu has a meatier texture than fresh tofu.

Pressed tofu Fresh tofu cubes are dried and pressed until they become firm cakes with a brown skin. Pressed tofu is sliced and added to stir-fries, and is especially popular during Buddhist festivals as it is regarded as a pure vegetarian food.

Fermented tofu Also known as preserved bean curd, fermented tofu is not used as a main ingredient, but more as a flavouring to marinate poultry or as a seasoning for braised dishes. It comes in two types: white and red. The red variety is more popular in Shanghai cuisine.

Tofu skins These flat, wrinkly sheets can crack easily, so they have to be moistened slightly before use. They can be used to wrap fillings into parcels in the same way spring roll wrappers are used. They have a superior taste to spring roll wrappers. They are made by boiling soya milk until a skin forms on top. This skin is then lifted off and dried.

Tofu wafers Light brown in colour and slightly sweet in taste, tofu wafers can be fried and then added as a garnish on noodles or stews. In Fujian cooking, they are often deep-fried and added to spring roll fillings for added crunch.

Fruit, nuts and seeds

In China, fruit tends to be eaten as a palate cleanser rather than being made into desserts. Many types of tropical fruit are grown and eaten in eastern China.

Banana One of the most widely eaten fruits in China, they are usually eaten fresh, but can also be fried.

Pineapple Ripe pineapples are eaten fresh, but they are also used as an ingredient in sweet and sour dishes.

Plum In China, plums are eaten fresh, pickled, dried and salted, as well as being used to make plum sauce.

Mango Several varieties of mango are available in eastern China. The skins can be yellow, pale orange or green, and the flesh is sweet and juicy.

Papaya Also known as pawpaw, this yellow-skinned fruit is popular in China.

Lime This citrus fruit is used fresh and preserved. It enhances flavours in marinades and can be used as a souring agent in soups.

Mandarin orange This type of orange has been cultivated for centuries and is traditional during New Year festivities. The skin is dried and used as a citrus seasoning in savoury and sweet dishes.

Jackfruit This large spiky fruit reveals a creamy and chewy flesh that tastes a little like ripe mango.

Lychee Sweet and fragrant, these tropical fruits are usually eaten as a refreshing snack, and are occasionally incorporated into savoury dishes.

Longan Grown widely in Fujian, this fruit comes in several varieties. They are used fresh when in season, but are also available canned and dried.

Persimmon Sometimes called Sharon fruit, these are often dried for use in herbal drinks.

Chinese dates These dates are usually sold with the stones (pits) in, but they are easy to remove with a sharp knife. They can be bought in dried form all year round and are used in sweet dishes.

Coconut Coconuts are shredded and squeezed to produce rich coconut milk that is used in sweet and savoury recipes.

Ginkgo nuts Popular in sweet and savoury dishes, ginkgo nuts can be bought vacuum-packed or canned, which saves the lengthy process of soaking and boiling them to make them tender. They are believed to have many health benefits and contain restorative nutrients.

Lotus seeds Like ginkgo nuts, dried lotus seeds require lengthy soaking and boiling before use, so it is best to buy them canned so that they are ready to use. They are added to sweet soups and other desserts.

Alcoholic drinks

In China, alcoholic drinks tend to be consumed between meals, rather than with meals. Wine from grapes is not traditional, although younger people are beginning to enjoy it due to greater Western influence in China.

Chinese grain wines Chinese wines are of two types: yellow (huang jiu) and white (mi jiu). The yellow type, which can be made from different grains, is fermented and becomes clear or yellowish-brown in colour. The white kind is distilled and made from glutinous rice.

Flavoured wines Many types of unusual flavoured wines are used in the cooking of eastern China. Mei Kuei Lu Chiew, literally, 'rose essence liquor', is a variety of Kaoliang wine from north China.

Distilled spirits The most famous spirit is Maotai, named after the village where it originated.

Above, left to right Lychees, Chinese red dates and green tea.

Tea

There are hundreds of varieties of tea, but they all fall into two types: black (or red) and green. Most black tea is produced in the Fujian province, and Zhejiang is the main producer of green tea. Famous teas include Jasmine, Oolong, Fujian Black, Gunpowder and Dragon Well Tea. Ingredients such as prawns (shrimp) are marinated in tea before being stir-fried, which gives the dish an intense flavour.

Shaoxing wine

This is China's most high-profile wine and is available all over the world. It originated in Shaoxing in Zhejiang and is made from glutinous rice. It is a fragrant wine and deep amber in colour. It is sometimes sold as Xiaoxing, and is used in many recipes from all over China, not just those of the eastern provinces.

Soups and dim sum

Throughout Chinese cuisine, soups are rarely regarded as a mere appetizer. It is traditional to serve a soup with the main meal as a refresher and to whet the appetite for what is still to come. While dim sum have become known as tasty snacks over the centuries, they often also appear as appetizers during special or festive meals. In everyday family dinners, one or more dim sum dishes may actually be served as a main course, especially the more substantial dumplings.

Versatile soups and dumplings

Eastern Chinese soups can range from the very light to broths of substance. Tofu and vegetables play important roles in the soup menu, with Shanghai offerings such as Tofu and Spinach Soup, for example. Pork, fish and shellfish are also favourite ingredients, especially in the hearty fare that is prepared during the winter months. In rural areas of eastern China, thick soups packed with seafood, meat, tofu and root vegetables are often served as evening meals in themselves. Soup bases are like blank canvases to which just about anything can be added. In eastern China, it is common for lard or white cooking fat to be added to soups, giving them a silky smooth feeling in the mouth.

Congee, or rice porridge, often falls into the dim sum category, even though it is not a dumpling. Salted Duck Egg Congee is one such example, served both in the eastern provinces and elsewhere in China. Pumpkin Cake and Steamed Prawn Dumplings are also typical eastern Chinese snacks. Today, most Chinese people consider eating at a dim sum restaurant a special treat, as few families are inclined to prepare so many small dishes at home. Most dim sum restaurants feature as many as 50 items on the menu. Many are fiddly to prepare and require skills learned over years of dim sum-making. The selection of recipes here will allow even the novice Chinese cook to create the stunning translucent dumplings at home.

Serves 4

150g/5oz spinach, preferably
   Chinese spinach, if available
800ml/27fl oz/scant 3¼ cups
   boiling water
75g/3oz salt fish
30ml/2 tbsp vegetable oil
2 garlic cloves, crushed
30ml/2 tbsp light soy sauce
2.5ml/½ tsp ground black pepper
15ml/1 tbsp sesame oil
115g/4oz tofu, cut into
   1cm/½in cubes

Tofu and spinach soup

Although Chinese spinach comes from the same botanical family as regular spinach, and is similar to it, it is more robust and fibrous in texture with purple streaks running all the way from the stem to the leaves. It is believed to be restorative for the blood. Chinese spinach is usually sold with the roots still on, and is becoming more easily available. Tofu is a centuries-old food appreciated for being high in protein and low in fat, as well as for its quality of blending with, and complementing, other ingredients. Salt fish is widely used in Shanghai cooking as a salting and flavouring agent.

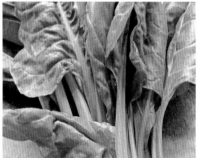

1 Tear the spinach leaves into small pieces and slice the stalks thinly. Set aside. Pour the boiling water into a large pan and return to the boil. Add the salt fish and simmer for 10 minutes.

2 Meanwhile, heat the oil in a small pan and fry the garlic for 30 seconds. Pour the garlic and oil into the stock and add the soy sauce, pepper and sesame oil.

3 Simmer for 2 minutes, then add the tofu and spinach. Cook for 2 minutes and serve hot.

Variation If salt fish is not to your liking, soak 15ml/1 tbsp dried shrimps or anchovies and add to the soup.

Per portion Energy 150kcal/620kJ; Protein 7g; Carbohydrate 2g, of which sugars 1g; Fat 13g, of which saturates 2g; Cholesterol 6mg; Calcium 215mg; Fibre 2g; Sodium 628mg.

Carp and mooli soup

The people of Shanghai are famously skilled at preparing and cooking seafood, because the delta and coastal regions of eastern China are prolific with fish and shellfish of every imaginable type. Carp are prized for their ornamental beauty, symbolism (gold and silver carp are believed to be the bringers of good fortune), and wonderful taste and texture. Whenever there is a meal requiring fish, the bones and carcass are not discarded but instead simmered with aromatics to make a stock for another day. It is easier, however, to use a fish stock cube.

1 Heat the oil in a wok, add the garlic and ginger, and fry until golden brown. Drain, reserving the oil, and set the garlic and ginger aside. Cut the carp into 5mm/¼in thick slices.

2 Pour the water into a large pan and add the stock cube. Bring back to the boil and add the reserved garlic and ginger oil, the carp and radish. Simmer for 5 minutes, then add the soy sauce, sesame oil and pepper.

3 Simmer for 3 minutes, then serve hot, garnished with the fried garlic and ginger, and fresh coriander leaves.

Variation Any firm-fleshed fish, such as halibut, cod or haddock, can also be used.

Serves 4

30ml/2 tbsp vegetable oil
3 garlic cloves, roughly chopped
25g/1oz ginger, peeled and shredded
300g/11oz carp fillets
800ml/27fl oz/scant 3¼ cups
  boiling water
1 fish stock (bouillon) cube
150g/5oz mooli (daikon) or white
  radish, cut into 1cm/½in cubes
30ml/2 tbsp light soy sauce
30ml/2 tbsp sesame oil
2.5ml/½ tsp ground black pepper
fresh coriander (cilantro) leaves,
  to garnish

Per portion Energy 215kcal/894kJ; Protein 16g; Carbohydrate 3g, of which sugars 2g; Fat 16g, of which saturates 2g; Cholesterol 50mg; Calcium 100mg; Fibre 1g; Sodium 873mg.

Fish ball noodle soup

A dish with a long history and peasant beginnings, fish ball noodles have earned a rightful place as comfort food. This noodle soup is sold by hawkers all over China and South-east Asia. Although it originated in this region, it is now an established item on the menus of Chinese restaurants across the globe. Traditionally regarded as a late-night supper dish, it has been known to soothe the hunger pangs of mahjong players, who clatter their tiles through the night in Hong Kong, Singapore, New York and other places around the world.

1 Soak the mung bean noodles in warm water for about 15 minutes until they swell and become gelatinous. Drain. Pour the boiling water into a large pan, add the stock cube and bring back to the boil. Add the fish balls, and boil for 5 minutes. They will swell slightly and become a little crunchy.

2 Add the noodles and simmer for 3 minutes, then add all the other ingredients. Garnish with coriander leaves. Serve with sliced red or green chillies and light soy sauce, allowing each diner to add them to taste.

Serves 4

150g/5oz mung bean noodles
800ml/27fl oz/scant 3¼ cups
  boiling water
1 fish stock (bouillon) cube
24 store-bought fish balls
15ml/1 tbsp light soy sauce
15g/½oz/1 tbsp preserved winter
  vegetable (tung choy)
2.5ml/½ tsp ground black pepper
15ml/1 tbsp sesame oil
2 spring onions (scallions), chopped
fresh coriander (cilantro) leaves,
  to garnish
sliced red or green chillies and light
  soy sauce, to serve

Per portion Energy 375 kcal/1558kJ; Protein 20g; Carbohydrate 49g, of which sugars 7g; Fat 10g, of which saturates 7g; Cholesterol 100mg; Calcium 273mg; Fibre 1g; Sodium 2285mg.

Serves 4

800ml/27fl oz/scant 3¼ cups meat
  stock or water
115g/4oz ham, diced into
  1cm/½in cubes
150g/5oz young bamboo shoots,
  cut into thin strips
30ml/2 tbsp vegetable oil
2 garlic cloves, crushed
30ml/2 tbsp Shaoxing wine
  or dry sherry
30ml/2 tbsp light soy sauce
5ml/1 tsp lard or white cooking fat
1 egg, lightly beaten
25g/1oz/¼ cup peas, thawed
  if frozen

Cook's tip Adding a little lard or
white cooking fat to soups is a
particular Chinese practice that
makes soups 'smooth'. This alludes
to the silky feeling on the throat
when you swallow it, rather than to
the texture.

Per portion Energy 173kcal/715kJ; Protein 10g;
Carbohydrate 2g, of which sugars 1g; Fat 14g,
of which saturates 3g; Cholesterol 83mg;
Calcium 20mg; Fibre 1g; Sodium 896mg.

Ham and bamboo shoot soup

*This fragrant soup hails from Hangzhou in Zhejiang Province, which has
been known as a popular beauty spot for centuries. There is an old
Chinese saying: 'In Heaven there is Paradise; in China we have Hangzhou.'
This beautiful city also offers many gastronomic delights. Chinese ham is
very different from the Western kind and the best is reputed to come
from Jinhua, also in the same province. If this is unavailable, use any
flavoursome smoked ham. The equally illustrious Shaoxing wine also
comes from the province of Zhejiang.*

1 Put the stock or water into a large pan and bring to the boil. Add the ham and bamboo
shoots, and simmer for 15 minutes.

2 Heat the oil in a small pan and fry the garlic for 30 seconds, then pour the garlic and oil
into the stock. Add the wine or sherry, soy sauce and lard. Simmer for 2 minutes.

3 Swirl the beaten egg into the stock mixture and stir until the stock is streaked with the
egg. Add the peas and cook for 2 minutes.

Serves 4

800ml/27fl oz/scant 3¹/₄ cups
  boiling water
115g/4oz/³/₄ cup processed soya
  beans, soaked overnight,
  rinsed and drained
150g/5oz/generous ¹/₂ cup minced
  (ground) pork
30ml/2 tbsp vegetable oil
2 garlic cloves, crushed
15ml/1 tbsp yellow bean sauce
2.5ml/¹/₂ tsp ground black pepper
15ml/1 tbsp sesame oil
2.5ml/¹/₂ tsp sugar
2 spring onions (scallions), chopped
coriander (cilantro) leaves, to garnish

Cook's tip You can also use dried,
unprocessed soya beans. Soak them
overnight, then boil them rapidly for
30 minutes and then simmer for
1–2 hours until cooked. Let the beans
cool, then rub them in your hands to
remove the skins. Use them in the
same way as the processed beans.

Minced pork and soya bean soup

*Soya beans grow profusely throughout most of China and, when not used
to make tofu, are cooked much like normal pulses. Chinese stores sell
them dried and they have to be soaked overnight, but many stores also
sell processed soya beans that require no soaking. They are frequently
used as a stock base because they impart a distinctive, almost meaty,
flavour. Soya beans are also extremely nutritious, being rich in protein.
Yellow bean sauce is used here as a salting agent that gives a smoky
flavour to the soup and complements the soya bean stock.*

1 Pour the boiling water into a large pan and add the soya beans. Bring to the boil and
simmer for 15 minutes. Break up the minced pork with a fork, then add to the stock so that
it forms lumps when it comes in contact with the boiling liquid.

2 Simmer for 5 minutes, then add all the other ingredients except the spring onions. Cook
for 3 minutes and, just before serving, add the spring onions. Serve, garnished with coriander.

Per portion Energy 242kcal/1101kJ; Protein 15g;
Carbohydrate 16g, of which sugars 2g; Fat 14g,
of which saturates 2g; Cholesterol 24mg;
Calcium 31mg; Fibre 4g; Sodium 132mg.

Spare rib and bitter melon soup

Bitter melon, or bitter gourd, is recommended by Chinese herbalists as an antidote to many ills, principally as a blood-pressure moderator and a kidney cleanser. However, any food with a bitter element is regarded in this way. When cooking, chefs recommend that you can temper some of the bitterness by steeping cut slices in a little salt and then squeezing out the moisture. Fujian bitter-melon lovers, however, would never do such a thing, as it is the very bitterness of the melon that is its intrinsic allure. It would be rather like removing the mould from Stilton!

1 Cut the pork ribs into 2.5cm/1in pieces. Cut the bitter melon lengthways and remove and discard the soft core and red seeds. Scrape away and discard any white pith that clings to the green flesh. Cut the flesh into half-moon slices, 1cm/½in wide.

2 Pour the boiling water into a large pan, add the pork rib pieces and simmer for 45 minutes, until the meat comes away from the bones easily (simmer for a further 15 minutes if the ribs are not tender enough). The stock will reduce to about 800ml/ 27fl oz/scant 3¼ cups. Skim off any fatty froth floating on top.

3 Add the remaining ingredients (except for the chilli sauce) and simmer for 5 minutes. Serve with a side dish of chilli sauce in which to dip the pork ribs and bitter melon.

Serves 4

300g/11oz meaty pork ribs
1 bitter melon
1.2 litres/2 pints/5 cups boiling water
30ml/2 tbsp light soy sauce
2.5ml/½ tsp ground black pepper
15g/½oz/1 tbsp dried shrimps,
   soaked until soft, minced (ground)
2.5ml/½ tsp sugar
5ml/1 tsp lard or white cooking fat
chilli sauce, for dipping

Variation If you are short of time, use fairly lean pork, thinly sliced, instead of ribs. Cook it for 30 minutes before adding the other ingredients.

Per portion Energy 181kcal/755kJ; Protein 18g; Carbohydrate 2g, of which sugars 1g; Fat 12g, of which saturates 4g; Cholesterol 70mg; Calcium 72mg; Fibre 3g; Sodium 771mg.

Salted duck egg congee

A watery rice porridge, congee has been a staple dish throughout China and South-east Asia for centuries. The word congee is believed to have derived from the Dravidian word 'kanji' (an Indian rice porridge). Its history is rooted in peasant farming communities where a little rice had to feed many people. Over time many things have been thrown into the congee pan – from vegetables to salt fish, eggs and meat. Today, expensive ingredients like lobster, scallops and oysters are added. True congee uses broken rice, which is available in Chinese stores.

1 Bring the rice and 1 litre/1³/₄ pints/4 cups water to the boil and simmer for 30 minutes, or until the rice grains are mushy and the liquid is milky. If the consistency is too thick, add more boiling water.

2 Hard-boil the salted duck eggs for 10 minutes. Cool in cold water, then peel off the shells. Cut into quarters.

3 Set aside four of the duck egg quarters and half the chopped spring onions for garnishing, then add the rest and all of the other ingredients to the rice porridge. Bring to a gentle boil over low heat. Cook for a further 5 minutes, or until well incorporated. Remove from the heat and allow to cool a little before serving warm. Garnish each dish with the reserved spring onions and a quarter of duck egg. Sprinkle with a little extra white pepper and serve.

Variation This simple but warming dish can be dressed up by adding cooked minced (ground) pork, salt fish or chicken – in fact, anything you fancy.

Serves 4

100g/3³/₄oz/¹/₂ cup broken rice
2 salted duck eggs
5ml/1 tsp preserved winter
  vegetable (tung choy)
15ml/1 tbsp sesame oil
5ml/1 tsp salt
5ml/1 tsp white pepper,
  plus extra to serve
2 spring onions (scallions), chopped

Per portion Energy 192kcal/809kJ; Protein 7g; Carbohydrate 22g, of which sugars 0g; Fat 9g, of which saturates 2g; Cholesterol 255mg; Calcium 45mg; Fibre 1g; Sodium 547mg.

Makes 8 pieces

4 quail's eggs, hard-boiled
4 slices of white bread,
   crusts removed
2 eggs, lightly beaten
250g/9oz/generous 1 cup minced
   (ground) pork
15ml/1 tbsp light soy sauce
2.5ml/½ tsp white pepper
5ml/1 tsp cornflour (cornstarch)
sesame seeds, for coating
vegetable oil, for deep-frying
sliced cucumber and hoisin sauce
   or chilli sauce, to serve

Per portion Energy 171kcal/1713kJ; Protein 12g;
Carbohydrate 8g, of which sugars 1g; Fat 10g,
of which saturates 2g; Cholesterol 168mg;
Calcium 47g; Fibre 1g; Sodium 254mg.

Quail's egg sesame toast

Sesame toast is a favourite on dim sum menus and makes a good choice of finger food when entertaining. This recipe has a hard-boiled quail's egg sitting beneath the usual filling of minced pork. When coated with sesame seeds and deep-fried, these have an intriguing flavour and texture.

1 Put the quail's eggs in a pan of boiling water and cook for 5 minutes. Drain then cool in cold water. Shell the eggs and cut each in half.

2 Cut each slice of bread into two triangles. Brush with beaten egg. Mix the minced pork with the soy sauce, pepper and cornflour, stirring well.

3 Place a halved quail's egg, cut side down, on each bread triangle and spread minced pork over the top, patting it in firmly. Brush with beaten egg.

4 Spread a generous amount of sesame seeds over a plate and carefully coat the top of each covered toast liberally. Shake off the excess.

5 Heat the oil to 180°C/350°F (test by frying a small cube of bread; it should brown in 40 seconds) and fry the toasts until golden brown. Serve with sliced cucumber and hoisin sauce or chilli sauce, for dipping.

Variation You can also use minced (ground) chicken or prawns (shrimp) instead of pork.

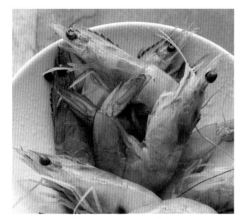

Sweet turnip dumplings

Also known as jicama, sweet turnips are similar in texture to the common swede (rutabaga) but with the sweetness of a conference pear and a hint of water chestnuts. They have a light tan-coloured skin and are shaped like spinning tops. The flesh is white and very crunchy, often used as a filling ingredient for spring rolls or stir-fried as a vegetable in the province of Fujian. Sweet turnips are not common outside of China, but they are sold fresh by some Chinese and Thai stores. Each dumpling should about 7.5cm/3in long, and half as wide.

1 To make the filling, cut the sweet turnip into matchstick strips about 5mm/¼in thick. Heat the oil and fry the garlic for 20 seconds, then add the yellow bean sauce, sugar, soy sauce and sesame oil. Stir for 30 seconds and then add the turnip and 500ml/17fl oz/2¼ cups water.

2 Simmer over medium heat for 25 minutes, or until nearly dry and the turnip pieces have broken up. Add the prawns and cook for 2 minutes. Allow to cool.

3 Mix the wheat starch, cornflour and salt together in a bowl and slowly add the hot water, stirring well to mix and form a soft dough. Add the oil and continue to knead a little until the mixture is the consistency of bread dough.

4 Roll out the dough into a cylinder shape on a board sprinkled with wheat starch. Cut into 12 equal pieces and form into sausage shapes. With a small rolling pin, flatten each piece into a round and roll out to 9cm/3½in in diameter.

5 Drain the turnip mixture well. Put one heaped tablespoonful of the mixture in the centre of a piece of dough. Fold in half to make a half-moon shape. Seal the edge with a little dab of water, and crimp. Trim off any floppy edges. Repeat with the other dough pieces.

6 Arrange the dumplings on a lightly oiled plate that will fit into your steamer and steam over a pan of boiling water for 15 minutes on high heat. The cooked dumplings will have a translucent and glossy appearance. Serve with a sweet soy sauce dip.

Makes about 10 dumplings

60g/2¼oz/generous ½ cup wheat
  starch, plus extra for dusting
75g/3oz/⅔ cup cornflour (cornstarch)
a pinch of salt
200ml/7fl oz/scant 1 cup hot water
15ml/1 tbsp vegetable oil
sweet soy sauce dip, to serve

For the filling
450g/1lb sweet turnip or
  jicama, peeled
30ml/2 tbsp vegetable oil
2 garlic cloves, crushed
15ml/1 tbsp yellow bean sauce
5ml/1 tsp sugar
15ml/1 tbsp light soy sauce
15ml/1 tbsp sesame oil
150g/5oz small prawns (shrimp),
  peeled and chopped

Variation In Guangdong, bamboo shoots are used instead of sweet turnip. Slice canned bamboo shoots into similar sized pieces as the turnip but cook them for 15 minutes.

Per portion Energy 130kcal/545kJ; Protein 3g; Carbohydrate 16g, of which sugars 3g; Fat 6g, of which saturates 1g; Cholesterol 29mg; Calcium 37g: Fibre 1g; Sodium 187mg.

Steamed prawn dumplings

The batter for these dumplings uses wheat starch (known as mien fen in Mandarin), mixed with cornflour or tapioca flour to achieve the exquisite translucence that typifies the pastry texture. It is an accepted fact that dim sum originated in South China, and any batter that steams to a translucent thinness is known as Ha Gau (Cantonese) pastry. The dough dries out quickly, so it needs to be filled and cooked immediately.

1 To make the filling, peel and wash the prawns and cut each into small dice. Mix the sugar and cornflour in a bowl and rub the prawn pieces gently in the mixture to coat thoroughly. Wash off the cornflour and sugar by putting the prawns in a colander and rinsing them under running water for 10 minutes. Drain well. This gives the prawns a delicious crunch.

2 In a bowl, combine the prawn pieces, spring onion, salt, sugar and pepper. Put into a pan and cook over a low heat for 5 minutes, stirring often, or until the prawns turn pink with a fairly thick coating. Allow to cool.

3 In a bowl, mix the wheat starch, cornflour and salt together, then slowly add the hot water, mixing well to form a soft dough. The consistency should be similar to bread dough but less springy.

4 Roll the dough into a cylinder shape on a board sprinkled with wheat starch flour. Cut into 20 equal pieces and form into sausage shapes. With a small rolling pin, flatten each piece into a round and roll out until about 7.5cm/3in in diameter and the thinness of parchment.

5 Put one heaped teaspoonful of prawn mixture into the centre of a piece of dough. Fold in half to make a half-moon shape. Pinch the ends together, then pleat and shape into a closed dumpling. Repeat with the other dough pieces.

6 Arrange the dumplings on a lightly oiled plate and steam over a pan of boiling water for 15 minutes on high heat. The cooked dumplings will have a glossy, pearly appearance. Serve with a soy sauce or chilli sauce dip.

Makes about 20

60g/2¹/₄oz/generous ¹/₂ cup wheat
  starch, plus extra for dusting
75g/3oz/²/₃ cup cornflour (cornstarch)
a pinch of salt
200ml/7fl oz/1 cup hot water
soy sauce dip or chilli sauce dip,
  to serve

For the filling
675g/1¹/₂lb prawns (shrimp)
5ml/1 tsp sugar
5ml/1 tsp cornflour (cornstarch)
1 spring onion (scallion),
  finely chopped
5ml/1 tsp salt
2.5ml/¹/₂ tsp sugar
2.5ml/¹/₂ tsp ground white pepper

Cook's tip

Wheat starch has a fine consistency, similar to that of cornflour (cornstarch). It is especially good for making dim sum dough and is widely available in Chinese stores.

Per dumpling Energy 52kcal/221kJ; Protein 6g; Carbohydrate 7g, of which sugars 0g; Fat 0g, of which saturates 0g; Cholesterol 66mg; Calcium 29g; Fibre 0g; Sodium 166mg.

Pumpkin cake

This delicious Fujian snack is often made during festive occasions. It is one of the most comforting foods on the eastern Chinese menu and a lovely way to use up pumpkin when all the Halloween madness is over. This is a savoury, and yet sweet, concoction that bears much similarity to the Yam Cake of South China, which is a more famous dim sum offering. It is usually served during Chinese New Year, but is a tempting mouthful on any day.

1 Steam the pumpkin for 20 minutes, or until soft enough to mash easily. Allow the pumpkin to cool, then process it to a fine paste using a food processor or potato masher.

2 Mix the rice flour, tapioca flour and mashed pumpkin together. Stir to mix thoroughly until the mixture is a smooth paste the consistency of thick batter.

3 Chop the soaked dried shrimps roughly. Snip off and discard the mushroom stems, then slice the caps.

4 Heat the oil in a wok and fry the garlic for 30 seconds until light brown. Add the dried shrimps, mushrooms and sausage, and fry for 1 minute. Add the sesame oil, soy sauce and pepper, and stir for 30 seconds until well mixed.

5 Mix well with the prepared pumpkin mash, making sure the ingredients are well distributed. Transfer to a lightly oiled steaming tray and press gently with a spatula to form a firm, round cake. Steam for 25 minutes or until cooked through. Allow to cool completely, then chill. Cut into wedges and serve with cucumber slices and a spicy dip.

Serves 6–8

1kg/2¼lb pumpkin, cut into chunks
300g/11oz/2⅔ cups rice flour
30ml/2 tbsp tapioca flour
50g/2oz dried shrimps, soaked and drained
8 Chinese dried mushrooms, soaked until soft
45ml/3 tbsp vegetable oil
4 garlic cloves, crushed
1 Chinese sausage, cut into very small dice
15ml/1 tbsp sesame oil
30ml/2 tbsp light soy sauce
2.5ml/½ tsp ground white pepper
sliced cucumber and a spicy dip, to serve

Per portion Energy 267kcal/1115kJ; Protein 8g; Carbohydrate 40g, of which sugars 2g; Fat 8g, of which saturates 1g; Cholesterol 32mg; Calcium 126g: Fibre 1g; Sodium 542mg.

Fish and shellfish

The coastal stretches of eastern China are rich in the fish and shellfish that underpin the cuisines of the entire region. Be they ocean or river catches, fish and shellfish appear as both basic sustenance and banquet dishes. Chefs, whether they are from Shanghai or tiny villages, are proud of their skills in preparing the freshwater and saltwater hauls. Maximum flavour is achieved through reverential treatment with well-balanced aromatics and seasonings.

Steamed, smoked, braised or fried

In this region of abundant fish and shellfish, chefs regard each type of fish as distinct when pairing it with flavourings and cooking methods. Robust fish like carp, eel, pomfret and porgy are popular, as they can withstand aromatics and seasonings that maximize their flavour. The coastal regions that stretch from Jiangsu to Fujian yield a magnificent array of these types of fish, and they are typically combined with bold ingredients like black bean sauce.

In Hangzhou, chefs are insistent on using only fish from the famous West Lake, as they believe the quality to be unbeatable. Dishes such as West Lake Fish in Vinegar Sauce demonstrate this penchant for local products. When cooking this dish at home, you can use any good fresh fish.

Rice wine is used in many of the fish recipes of the region, with Shaoxing wine from Zhejiang being the most popular. It adds wonderful depth of flavour to fish and shellfish dishes.

Excess fish is transformed into delightful morsels, such as fish balls, which can be added to many a dish. These can be bought from Chinese stores along with a whole host of other processed fish shapes. They can also be made at home, such as in the recipe for Fried Prawn Balls, and these have a superior flavour to store-bought ones.

Crab meat is combined with tofu for the Huaiyang dish of Braised Tofu with Crab, which is a dish of peasant origin that has been transformed to make it fit for emperors.

Serves 4

Serves 4

600g/1lb 5oz monkfish or any
  firm-fleshed fish, filleted
15ml/1 tbsp cornflour (cornstarch),
  plus 5ml/1 tsp for the sauce
vegetable oil, for deep-frying
30g/1¼oz cloud ear (wood ear)
  mushrooms, soaked in cold water
  for 20 minutes
30ml/2 tbsp vegetable oil
2 garlic cloves, chopped
25g/1oz fresh root ginger,
  peeled and chopped
15ml/1 tbsp oyster sauce
15ml/1 tbsp hoisin sauce
30ml/2 tbsp Chinese wine
2.5ml/½ tsp ground white or
  black pepper
chopped Chinese celery leaves,
  to garnish

Seaweed fish

The seaweed reference in the name of this dish is misleading, as no seaweed is used, though the thinly sliced cloud ears, once cooked, do resemble seaweed in texture. Many Chinese dishes, like this one, have names that are mystifyingly not reflected in the ingredients used. It is usually the result of symbolism, which plays a large part in Chinese culinary culture.

1 Cut the fish into 2.5cm/1in chunks and coat with 15ml/1 tbsp cornflour. Dust off the excess. Heat the oil for deep-frying in a wok or deep-fryer. Deep-fry the fish until golden. Set aside.

2 Using scissors, trim off any hard woody parts from the cloud ears and cut into fine strips. Heat 30ml/2 tbsp oil in a wok and fry the garlic and ginger for 30 seconds until golden brown. Add the oyster sauce, hoisin sauce, wine, 175ml/6fl oz/¾ cup water and the pepper, and bring to the boil.

3 Add the fish and simmer for 3 minutes, or until nearly cooked. Add the cloud ears and simmer for 2 minutes more.

4 Blend the 5ml/1 tsp cornflour with a little water and add it to the pan to thicken the sauce. Stir until well blended, then serve, garnished with Chinese celery leaves.

Per portion Energy 238kcal/1002kJ; Protein 25g; Carbohydrate 11g, of which sugars 0g; Fat 11g, of which saturates 1g; Cholesterol 21mg; Calcium 23g: Fibre 1g; Sodium 345mg.

Fish in black bean sauce

One of the most basic dishes in the Yangtze delta region is fish cooked in a black bean sauce. Black beans have been a staple seasoning in China for centuries. They are used whole, as fermented beans or processed into a rich, aromatic paste with ginger and garlic. Commercial black bean paste comes in many grades, some with Sichuan peppercorns and others with chilli. It has an affinity with sesame oil and spring onions.

1 Cut the fish into 2.5cm/1in cubes and rub with the salt. Wash and drain, then coat with cornflour. Shake off the excess. Heat the oil for deep-frying in a wok or deep-fryer and deep-fry the fish until crisp and golden brown. Set aside.

2 To make the sauce, heat 15ml/1 tbsp of the deep-frying oil in a wok and stir-fry the garlic and ginger for 40 seconds. Add the spring onion, black bean sauce, sugar, sesame oil, vinegar and 300ml/½ pint/1¼ cups water.

3 Cook for 1 minute, or until well blended, then add the fish. Stir over high heat for 2 minutes, or until the sauce is thick. Serve with boiled rice, garnished with chopped spring onions.

Serves 4

450g/1lb monkfish or halibut fillets
5ml/1 tsp salt
30ml/2 tbsp cornflour (cornstarch)
vegetable oil, for deep-frying

For the sauce
2 garlic cloves, crushed
25g/1oz fresh root ginger,
  peeled and shredded
1 spring onion (scallion), chopped,
  plus extra to garnish
15ml/1 tbsp black bean sauce
5ml/1 tsp sugar
30ml/2 tbsp sesame oil
5ml/1 tsp vinegar, preferably Chinese
  rice wine vinegar
boiled rice, to serve

Variation You can omit the deep-frying stage and add the fish directly to the sauce to braise instead.

Per portion Energy 272kcal/1137kJ; Protein 18g;
Carbohydrate 10g, of which sugars 2g; Fat 18g,
of which saturates 2g; Cholesterol 16mg;
Calcium 19g: Fibre 0g; Sodium 611mg.

Wine-braised fish and leek

From Fuzhou comes a unique product called wine lees – the residual yeast from the wine-making process that produces a vivid crimson colour. It is added to many stews and seafood dishes. Although rather hard to come by, some Chinese stores do sell it. Alternatively, you can use a combination of preserved red bean curd (tofu ru) and wine for a flavour that is not too dissimilar. Leeks are eaten in China for their crunchy texture and pungent taste as well as for their symbolic representation of good fortune; the vegetable's Chinese name rhymes with the word for 'counting'.

1 Clean the fish and trim off any protruding sharp fins and the tail. Make several deep cuts along the deepest part of the body. Rub with salt. Dust with 15ml/1 tbsp cornflour and shake off the excess. Heat the oil for deep-frying in a wok or deep-fryer, then deep-fry the fish until crisp. Drain, set aside and keep warm.

2 Heat the 30ml/2 tbsp vegetable oil in a wok and fry the ginger and garlic for 30 seconds until golden brown. Add the sesame oil, then add the wine lees or bean curd and wine mixture. Add the soy sauce and stir for 1 minute over medium heat.

3 Add the leek, 300ml/¹⁄₂ pint/1¹⁄₄ cups water and the sugar, and quickly bring to the boil. Blend the remaining cornflour with a little water and stir it into the sauce until smooth and slightly thick. Add the whole fish and bathe liberally with the sauce for 30 seconds, or until heated through. Serve with a garnish of fried garlic or shallots.

Variation If you prefer, fish fillets deep-fried in the same way will work just as well.

Serves 4

2 red mullet or snapper, about
  675g/1¹⁄₂lb total weight
2.5ml/¹⁄₂ tsp salt
30ml/2 tbsp cornflour (cornstarch)
vegetable oil, for deep-frying
30ml/2 tbsp vegetable oil
25g/1oz fresh root ginger, peeled
  and shredded
4 garlic cloves, sliced
15ml/1 tbsp sesame oil
15ml/1 tbsp Fuzhou wine lees,
  or 1 cube preserved red bean
  curd (tofu ru) mashed with
  30ml/2 tbsp Chinese wine
15ml/1 tbsp light soy sauce
1 leek, white part only, thinly sliced
5ml/1 tsp sugar
fried slices of garlic or shallots,
  to garnish

Per portion Energy 302kcal/1269kJ; Protein 36g; Carbohydrate 11g, of which sugars 4g; Fat 13g, of which saturates 2g; Cholesterol 62mg; Calcium 91g: Fibre 1g; Sodium 648mg.

Smoked pomfret

Although traditionally a Sichuan style of food preparation, smoking has spread to all regions over time, and in Shanghai it is fairly common. Tea leaves are common smoking materials, as they give a subtle, smoky flavour that works well with seafood. Semi-fermented oolong tea from Fujian Province gives the best flavour. Pomfret belongs to the angel fish family and can grow as large as a dinner plate in the coastal waters of the eastern provinces. It is a flat fish, pale grey in colour, with delicate flesh and fine bones. There are two types, white and black, but the former is used here.

1 Rub the pomfret with the salt. Line a large wok with a double sheet of foil. To make the smoking mixture, mix the tea leaves with the flour and sugar, and spread evenly on top of the foil. Place a lightly oiled bamboo steamer on the wok, leaving space between the smoking materials and fish.

2 Put the pomfret directly on the steamer rack. Turn the heat to high and, when the smoke begins to appear, turn the heat down to medium. Smoke for 30 minutes. Remove the fish and leave to cool.

3 Drizzle with wine or sherry and sesame oil, and sprinkle the ginger over the top. Put on a deep plate in a bamboo steamer and steam for 10 minutes.

Variation If you cannot obtain pomfret, you can use snapper or porgy.

Serves 4

1 pomfret or porgy, about
  675g/1½lb, cleaned, with fins
5ml/1 tsp salt
vegetable oil, for greasing
45ml/3 tbsp Shaoxing wine or
  dry sherry
30ml/2 tbsp sesame oil
25g/1oz fresh root ginger, peeled and
  very thinly sliced

For the smoking materials
50g/2oz loose-leaf tea of your choice
150g/5oz/1¼ cups plain
  (all-purpose) flour
45ml/3 tbsp light muscovado (brown)
  or demerara (raw) sugar

Cook's tip There are usually three steps involved in smoked dishes: smoking, steaming and deep-frying. This normally applies to duck and tougher cuts of meat but not to delicate seafood, which is merely smoked then steamed.

Per portion Energy 185kcal/776kJ; Protein 23g; Carbohydrate 1g, of which sugars 0g; Fat 10g, of which saturates 2g; Cholesterol 46mg; Calcium 93g; Fibre 0g; Sodium 610mg.

Serves 4

600g/1lb 5oz carp or other whole
  firm-fleshed fish, cleaned
750ml/1¼ pints/3 cups boiling water
25g/1oz fresh root ginger,
  peeled and chopped
30ml/2 tbsp Shaoxing wine or
  dry sherry
30ml/2 tbsp dark soy sauce
5ml/1 tsp sugar
½ leek, white part only, thinly sliced
15ml/1 tbsp rice vinegar
15ml/1 tbsp cornflour (cornstarch)

Cook's tip You can also deep-fry the
carp instead of boiling it. Make the
sauce following step 3 onwards.

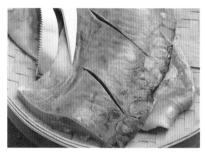

Per portion Energy 209kcal/880kJ; Protein 27g;
Carbohydrate 8g, of which sugars 2g; Fat 7g,
of which saturates 1g; Cholesterol 101mg;
Calcium 78g; Fibre 0g; Sodium 603mg.

West Lake fish in vinegar sauce

Hangzhou restaurant chefs are purists and will only serve fish caught from the famous West Lake. The Chinese also make a fine distinction between freshwater and saltwater fish, not on the premise that one is better than the other, but that there is an intrinsic difference in taste. Freshwater fish tend to lurk in muddy waters, so they are usually left to swim in tanks for a few days once caught, to temper their slightly muddy flavour. The most popular West Lake fish is the grass carp or mirror carp, which has a delicate flavour. You can use any fresh, quality fish available at your local fishmonger's.

1 With a sharp knife, slit all the way down the fish from the gills to the tail and open out to make a butterfly shape, one half with the bone and the other without. Cut deep slits along the thickest parts of the flesh on the skin side but not all the way to the bone.

2 Pour the boiling water into a wok and bring back to the boil. Lower in the whole fish and cook for 2 minutes, then lift out carefully with a slotted spoon and put on a serving plate.

3 Remove all but 200ml/7fl oz/scant 1 cup of the water and add the ginger, wine or sherry and the soy sauce. Cook for 1 minute, then add the sugar, leek and rice vinegar. Cook for 1 minute more.

4 Blend the cornflour with a little water, then stir into the wok and cook until the sauce is slightly thickened. Ladle over the boiled fish.

Fish and shellfish 49

Serves 4

1 large meaty fish head, such as
  tuna or salmon
30ml/2 tbsp vegetable oil
3 garlic cloves, chopped
25g/1oz fresh root ginger,
  peeled and chopped
15ml/1 tbsp black bean sauce
800ml/27fl oz/scant 3¼ cups
  boiling water
45ml/3 tbsp Chinese rose-flavoured
  wine (mei kwei lo)
a small piece of tangerine peel,
  about 5cm/2in square
a pinch of Chinese five-spice powder
2.5ml/½ tsp ground black pepper
200g/7oz cabbage leaves, shredded
4 spring onions (scallions),
  cut into 5cm/2in lengths
salt

Fish head casserole

Westerners not used to it might find the idea of eating fish heads unusual. To the Chinese, a fish head is as good as any part of the main body, as it contains a lot of tender meat, especially if the head is large. The best heads to use are salmon or tuna, but they have to weigh in at around 1kg/2¼lb to be worthy of being cooked. The meat yield is about a third of the actual weight, and is mostly found in the bulbous cheeks and near the gills.

1 Remove the gills and any entrails and cut the fish head into two pieces using a cleaver. Rub all over with salt, wash and drain.

2 Heat the oil in a wok and fry the garlic and ginger for 40 seconds, then add the black bean sauce. Stir for 1 minute, then add the boiling water, wine, tangerine peel, Chinese five-spice powder and pepper.

3 Bring to the boil and cook over a high heat for 5 minutes to reduce the liquid and concentrate the flavour. Add the cabbage and cook over high heat for 5 minutes.

4 Add the fish head and cook for another 10 minutes over medium heat. Add the spring onions and cook for a further 3 minutes, then serve.

Cook's tip The best way to serve this dish is in a preheated clay pot, if you have one, or a large casserole warmed in a hot oven.

Per portion Energy 236kcal/978kJ; Protein 18g; Carbohydrate 3g, of which sugars 2g; Fat 17g, of which saturates 2g; Cholesterol 42mg; Calcium 65g: Fibre 2g; Sodium 137mg.

Serves 4

675g/1½lb prepared eels,
  bones removed
salt, for preparing the eels
15ml/1 tbsp cornflour (cornstarch)
vegetable oil, for shallow frying
30ml/2 tbsp vegetable oil
25g/1oz fresh root ginger,
  peeled and shredded
2 spring onions (scallions),
  cut into 5cm/2in lengths
30ml/2 tbsp Shaoxing wine or sherry
30ml/2 tbsp hoisin sauce
15ml/1 tbsp dark soy sauce
2.5ml/½ tsp salt
strips of red chillies, to garnish

Variation Monkfish has a similar firm
texture to eel and can also be cooked
this way. Flaky fish that break up easily
are not recommended for this dish.

Per portion Energy 446kcal/1855kJ; Protein 29g;
Carbohydrate 6g, of which sugars 2g; Fat 34g,
of which saturates 7g; Cholesterol 253mg;
Calcium 47g; Fibre 0g; Sodium 855mg.

Stir-fried eels in hoisin sauce

*The riverine and delta areas of eastern China abound with eels that,
because they are cartilaginous and boneless apart from the main
vertebrae, make good eating. Eel meat is often likened to tender chicken,
rather like monkfish. Eels should always be alive when bought as they
do not keep well otherwise. Chinese stores and fishmongers always
sell them from fish tanks, as few Chinese will eat eels that have been killed
and frozen earlier. They are rather difficult to prepare so ask your
fishmonger to gut them and cut them into chunks.*

1 Pat the eels dry with kitchen paper and rub with a little salt to remove some of the
slippery coating on the skins. Cut into 2.5cm/1in medallions. Wash and drain, then coat
with cornflour.

2 Heat a pan or wok with oil for shallow frying and fry the eel pieces for 1 minute, or until
they are half-cooked. Drain well on kitchen paper.

3 Heat 30ml/2 tbsp oil and fry the ginger for 40 seconds. Add the spring onions, stir for
30 seconds and add the eels. Stir over high heat for 1 minute, then add the wine or sherry,
hoisin sauce, soy sauce, 120ml/4fl oz/½ cup water and the salt.

4 Stir over high heat for 1 minute, or until the sauce is slightly thick and glossy. Serve
garnished with strips of red chillies.

  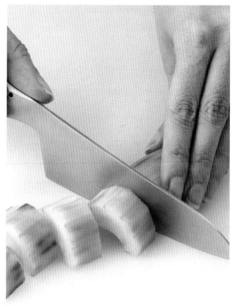

Fried fish balls

Fish balls are integral to the cuisine of Fujian, and Fuzhou chefs elevate the cooking of these delicacies to great heights. Being a coastal region, excess fish is processed into fish balls, fish cakes and pastes to be used as stuffing ingredients. Fish balls are often boiled or steamed, then fried and served with a sauce. Street food vendors sell this snack, often skewering a few on bamboo sticks. Fish balls are available in Chinese stores.

1 Bring a large pan of water to the boil and cook the fish balls for 5 minutes. Drain thoroughly and pat them dry on kitchen paper.

2 Heat the oil for deep-frying in a wok or deep-fryer and deep-fry the fish balls until golden brown. (When cooled, they will shrivel slightly.)

3 Blend together all of the sauce ingredients in a pan and warm gently over a low heat. Do not allow it to boil.

4 Peel and core the cucumber, then cut it into chunks, each the size of a fish ball.

5 Skewer the fish balls alternately with the cucumber, three fish balls and two pieces of cucumber to each skewer, and serve as a buffet item or snack with the sauce on the side. Alternatively, serve the fish balls in a deep plate mixed with the cucumber chunks and with the sauce poured over the top.

Cook's tip Chinese stores also sell prawn, squid and lobster balls, all of which can be cooked using the above method. They can also be simply boiled rather than fried and served with the sauce, if you prefer.

Serves 4 as an appetizer or 2 as a main dish

12 large prepared fish balls
vegetable oil, for deep-frying
$^1\!/_2$ cucumber

For the sauce
15ml/1 tbsp chilli sauce, or to taste
30ml/2 tbsp tomato ketchup
15ml/1 tbsp oyster sauce
45ml/3 tbsp water
5ml/1 tsp vinegar

Per portion Energy 212kcal/875kJ; Protein 10g; Carbohydrate 14g, of which sugars 7g; Fat 13g, of which saturates 4g; Cholesterol 50mg; Calcium 141g: Fibre 0g; Sodium 1398mg.

Fried prawn balls

Fujian chefs are very good at processing shellfish and fish into savoury balls and cakes for adding to noodle dishes. This recipe uses prawns, and the balls have a superlative flavour that makes them grand enough for banquets. The mixture needs a bit of work to achieve the correct consistency, but the resulting balls are superior to commercial ones, which tend to contain a lot of flour.

1 Process the prawns to a smooth paste in a blender or food processor. Transfer to a mortar and grind slowly with a pestle. As you do this, add the water and tapioca starch or cornflour a little at a time, turning the prawn paste as you work.

2 Add the salt, sesame oil and pepper, and blend well using the pestle. Continue to process the prawns in this way for at least 15 minutes. This will aerate the prawn mixture until it has a slightly springy texture. Alternatively, use a food processor or blender, although the results will not be quite the same, because of the cutting action of the blade rather than the grinding action of a pestle.

3 Using scissors, trim off and discard any hard woody parts from the cloud ears, then chop them finely. Add to the prawns and continue to process until well mixed.

4 With floured fingers, shape the mixture into small balls the size of large grapes. Heat the oil for deep-frying in a wok or deep-fryer. Deep-fry the prawn balls until golden brown, then remove and leave to cool. The balls will shrink a little, with slightly shrivelled skin; this is normal. Serve as an appetizer with chilli sauce for dipping.

Cook's tip
To devein a prawn, make a shallow cut down the centre of the curved back of the prawn. Pull out the black vein with a cocktail stick (toothpick) or your fingers. Rinse the prawn well.

Serves 4 as an appetizer

675g/1½lb prawns (shrimp), peeled
 and deveined (see Cook's Tip)
30ml/2 tbsp water
30ml/2 tbsp tapioca starch
 or cornflour (cornstarch),
 plus extra for dusting
5ml/1 tsp salt
15ml/1 tbsp sesame oil
2.5ml/½ tsp ground white pepper
25g/1oz cloud ear (wood ear)
 mushrooms, soaked in cold water
 for 20 minutes
vegetable oil, for deep-frying
chilli sauce, for dipping

Per portion Energy 252kcal/1054kJ; Protein 30g;
Carbohydrate 11g, of which sugars 0g; Fat 10g,
of which saturates 1g; Cholesterol 329mg;
Calcium 139g; Fibre 0g; Sodium 815mg.

Serves 4

450g/1lb large tiger prawns
  (jumbo shrimp), unpeeled
30ml/2 tbsp lard or white cooking fat,
  or vegetable oil
2.5ml/½ tsp salt
2 garlic cloves, crushed
25g/1oz fresh root ginger,
  peeled and shredded
1 spring onion (scallion), finely chopped
15ml/1 tbsp rice wine
5ml/1 tsp sugar
15ml/1 tbsp light soy sauce
5ml/1 tsp ground black pepper
shredded lettuce, to serve

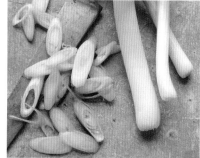

Dry-fried prawns

In Chinese cooking, there are many different types of stir-frying, ranging from flash-frying to 'fire in the wok' stir-frying. This traditional recipe from Anhui uses a dry stir-frying method, which is employed most often for delicate shellfish. For the best results, cook prawns in their shells with only the heads removed. It is traditional to use a little lard as the cooking agent instead of oil, to add extra flavour.

1 Wash the prawns, then remove the heads. Heat the lard or oil in a wok until very hot and stir-fry the prawns with the salt until they turn completely pink and glossy. Remove the prawns from the wok and set aside.

2 Add the garlic to the wok with the ginger and spring onion, and stir-fry for 1 minute. Add the rice wine, sugar, soy sauce and pepper, and stir to blend for 1 minute.

3 Return the prawns to the pan and toss until well coated. Serve on a bed of lettuce.

Cook's tip For a less oily dish, blanch the prawns in boiling water for 1 minute then cook as in steps 2 and 3, but use only 15ml/1 tbsp of lard or white cooking fat.

Per portion Energy 111kcal/464kJ; Protein 8g;
Carbohydrate 2g, of which sugars 2g; Fat 8g,
of which saturates 1g; Cholesterol 98mg;
Calcium 45g: Fibre 0g; Sodium 1076mg.

Phoenix prawns

This dish is believed to have been a creation of the Muslim Hui people, who number some 4.5 million and are scattered throughout the northern provinces. Their cuisine is regarded as a distinct entity, since Islam forbids the eating of pork, which is the main meat in China, and also alcohol. The name of the recipe is merely symbolic, because prawns, when cooked with their tails on, are likened to the mythical bird.

1 Peel the prawns, but leave the tails on. Devein the prawns by making a shallow cut down the centre of the curved back and pulling out the black vein.

2 Heat the oil in a pan or wok and fry the garlic for 20 seconds. Add the prawns and stir-fry for 1–2 minutes, or until they turn pink.

3 Add the soy sauce, sesame oil, peas and 90ml/6 tbsp water, and stir it begins to simmer.

4 Blend the cornflour with a little water and add to the pan. Stir for 1 minute, or until thick, and serve hot, with boiled rice, if you like.

Serves 4

450g/1lb large prawns (shrimp)
30ml/2 tbsp vegetable oil
2 garlic cloves, chopped
15ml/1 tbsp light soy sauce
15ml/1 tbsp sesame oil
30g/1¼oz/2 tbsp peas,
  thawed if frozen
5ml/1 tsp cornflour (cornstarch)
boiled rice, to serve (optional)

Variation Give the dish a little crunchiness by adding 30ml/ 2 tbsp of chopped water chestnuts, if you like.

Per portion Energy 117kcal/490kJ; Protein 9g; Carbohydrate 3g, of which sugars 0g; Fat 8g, of which saturates 1g; Cholesterol 98mg; Calcium 44g: Fibre 1g; Sodium 831mg.

Stir-fried prawns and ginkgo nuts

Ginkgo nuts come from the maidenhair tree and are regarded with near reverence for their restorative and medicinal properties; however, they also add flavour and a marvellous crunch to stir-fries and soups. Chinese stores sell them dried, canned or vacuum-packed. Dried ones take a long time to soak and soften, so it is best to use canned or vacuum-packed ones that need no preparation other than draining.

1 Devein the prawns by making a shallow cut down the centre of the curved back and pulling out the black vein. Cut the prawns into smaller pieces, if they are very large. Heat the oil in a wok and fry the garlic for 20 seconds, then add the spring onion. Stir for 30 seconds and add the oyster sauce, pepper and sesame oil.

2 Add the prawns and ginkgo nuts. Cook, stirring, for 2 minutes, until the prawns are cooked.

3 Blend 100ml/3½fl oz/scant ½ cup water with the cornflour and add it to the wok. Stir until the sauce is thick. Serve hot, garnished with spring onion and accompanied by noodles.

Serves 4

450g/1lb prawns (shrimp), shelled
15ml/1 tbsp vegetable oil
2 garlic cloves, chopped
1 spring onion (scallion), chopped
15ml/1 tbsp oyster sauce
2.5ml/½ tsp ground white or
  black pepper
15ml/1 tbsp sesame oil
24 vacuum-packed or canned ginkgo
  nuts, rinsed and drained
5ml/1 tsp cornflour (cornstarch)
chopped spring onion, to garnish
noodles, to serve

Per portion Energy 179kcal/749kJ; Protein 20g;
Carbohydrate 6g, of which sugars 0g; Fat 8g,
of which saturates 1g; Cholesterol 219mg;
Calcium 95g: Fibre 1g; Sodium 410mg.

Serves 4

450g/1lb prawns (shrimp), shelled
1 egg white
30ml/2 tbsp Shaoxing wine
  or dry sherry
2.5ml/½ tsp sugar
15ml/1 tbsp light soy sauce
5ml/1 tsp jasmine tea leaves
15ml/1 tbsp vegetable oil
1 spring onion (scallion), chopped,
  plus extra to garnish
2.5ml/½ tsp ground black pepper
15ml/1 tbsp sesame oil
boiled rice, to serve

Cook's tip Experiment with different Chinese teas such as lapsang souchong or pu erh, or even try Earl Grey for an unusual result.

Per portion Energy 169kcal/708kJ; Protein 21g; Carbohydrate 1g, of which sugars 1g; Fat 8g, of which saturates 1g; Cholesterol 219mg; Calcium 94g; Fibre 0g; Sodium 497mg.

Dragon Well prawns

The original version of this classic Hangzhou dish calls for the prawns to be cooked in Dragon Well tea, but it is something of an acquired taste as the tea flavour can be overpowering. Dragon Well tea is also hard to obtain outside China. Instead, use a weak tea made with jasmine tea leaves.

1 Devein the prawns by making a shallow cut down the centre of the curved back and pulling out the black vein. In a shallow dish, lightly beat the egg white and mix with the wine or sherry, sugar and soy sauce. Add the prawns and leave to marinate for 30 minutes.

2 Boil 250ml/8fl oz/1 cup water and brew the jasmine tea leaves for 3 minutes, then strain. Lift the prawns from their marinade and steep in the hot tea for 10 minutes, then drain.

3 Heat the oil in a wok and fry the spring onion for 30 seconds. Add the pepper and sesame oil. Stir for 30 seconds, then add the prawns and cook for 1–2 minutes, or until they are pink.

4 Drizzle a little of the marinade over and stir quickly for 20 seconds to blend. Serve garnished with chopped spring onions, on a bed of boiled rice.

Braised tofu with crab

From the Huaiyang school of cooking comes this delicate dish of crab and tofu that is typical of the region. It is a clay-pot dish believed to have peasant origins. It uses dried bamboo pith, which, when cooked, imparts a crunchy texture in contrast to the soft tofu and crab meat. The seasonings are a subtle mixture of yellow bean sauce, wine and hoisin sauce. If you do not have time to prepare fresh crab, use good quality canned crab meat.

1 Cut the tofu into 2.5cm/1in cubes. Heat the oil in a wok or deep-fryer until smoking, then lower the tofu pieces into the oil, one at a time, and deep-fry until a brown skin forms. Lift out with a slotted spoon and set aside.

2 Heat 15ml/1 tbsp oil in a large pan and fry the garlic for 20 seconds. Add the rice wine, yellow bean sauce and hoisin sauce, and stir for 30 seconds.

3 Cut the bamboo pith into short lengths about 4cm/1½in wide. Add to the pan with 350ml/12fl oz/1½ cups water and simmer for 3 minutes. Add the tofu and lightly beaten egg, and stir for 1 minute, or until the sauce is slightly thick.

4 Add the crab meat and stir for 30 seconds to heat through. Serve hot.

Cook's tips

• Scallops can also be cooked in the same way. Use frozen or fresh from the shell.

• If bamboo pith is not available, use ordinary canned bamboo shoots.

Serves 4

450g/1lb tofu, rinsed and drained
vegetable oil, for deep-frying
15ml/1 tbsp vegetable oil
2 garlic cloves, chopped
30ml/2 tbsp rice wine
15m/1 tbsp yellow bean sauce
15ml/1 tbsp hoisin sauce
75g/3oz bamboo pith,
  soaked until soft
1 egg, lightly beaten
350g/12oz white crab meat

Per portion Energy 472kcal/1966kJ; Protein 46g; Carbohydrate 4g, of which sugars 2g; Fat 30g, of which saturates 2g; Cholesterol 121mg; Calcium 1684g: Fibre 1g; Sodium 592mg.

Poultry

Throughout China, poultry always makes up a large proportion of the menu, with chicken and duck recipes being popular in every province. In Shanghai and the eastern provinces, chicken is occasionally cooked whole, which is relatively rare in much of China. The majority of dishes, however, use chicken in bitesize pieces, ready for people to help themselves during family meals. Chefs are skilled at matching the perfect spices to chicken and duck to create wonderful marriages of flavour in their stews and stir-fries.

Symbolic stews and culinary icons

From the bustling metropolis of Shanghai to the rural villages of Jiangxi and the humid port of Amoy, cooks in eastern China have created many dishes that have since become global culinary icons. Beggar's Chicken is an almost mystical concoction that has stood the test of time over many centuries. There is even a dish that has the Mandarin seal of approval: Prime Minister's Chicken Stew.

Stews and braised dishes are popular on the menus of the eastern provinces, especially during the colder winter months. Chicken, high in nutritional value, is paired with restorative ginseng in a truly warming, healthy and flavourful dish, Chicken and Ginseng Stew.

Marinated Duck is one of the stars of Zhejiang's poultry menu, with its deep flavour that develops from lengthy marinating. Even the simple dish Stir-fried Diced Chicken from Jiangxi cannot fail to impress, its fiery promise coming from a touch of chillies borrowed from neighbouring Hunan.

Whether it is the simplest or the most elaborate dish, a marriage of flavours and textures is the key to poultry perfection in eastern China. The art of cooking chicken and duck has been handed down from generation to generation, and through centuries of imperial and home cooking. Today, in the hands of cooks and chefs who understand the importance of this culinary synergy, there is no such thing as an ordinary dish, no matter how simple or complex the ingredients and method.

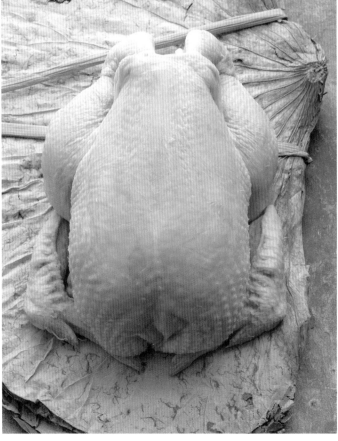

Beggar's chicken

The story behind this curiously named dish is about a vagrant who stole a chicken. Being fearful of being discovered, he decided to wrap it in lotus leaves and wet mud before flinging the whole parcel into a fire he had made to warm himself. In reality, this method of cooking has been around for centuries, especially in Micronesia, and it still exists in New Zealand and other Pacific islands. The recipe no longer calls for mud, of course, but uses a dough instead. The dough is edible but is not meant to be eaten. The beggar could not possibly have afforded the stuffing!

1 To make the dough wrapping, sift the flour into a mixing bowl, add the yeast, sugar, salt, water and egg whites, and mix to form a dough. Cover and leave to stand for 15 minutes, then knead for 5–6 minutes, or until the dough is soft and elastic. Leave to rise in a warm place for 1½–2 hours, or until doubled in size. Meanwhile, make the stuffing.

2 Soak the shiitake mushrooms for 20 minutes in at least 150ml/¼ pint/⅔ cup warm water, then strain, reserving the soaking liquid. Snip off and discard the stems. Thinly slice the caps. Soak the dried vegetable in cold water for 10 minutes, then rinse, squeeze dry and chop finely.

3 Heat the oil in a wok over high heat. Fry the ginger, garlic and onion for 20 seconds, add the chopped dried vegetable and fry for 1 minute. Add the minced pork or chicken, carrot, mushrooms, spring onions, soy sauce, wine or sherry and fry vigorously for 1 minute, then add 150ml/¼ pint/⅔ cup of the reserved mushroom soaking liquid. Cook for 1 minute more, then transfer to a bowl to cool. Stir in the sesame oil and pepper.

4 Preheat the oven to 200°C/400°F/Gas 6 and line a large roasting pan with foil. Rub the inside and outside of the chicken with wine and salt. Wipe down each lotus leaf with kitchen paper dipped in hot water to soften it.

5 Spoon the stuffing into the chicken, packing it in well. Secure the open end with string or sturdy wooden cocktail sticks (toothpicks). Wrap the chicken in the first lotus leaf as you would a parcel, then place seam side down on the second lotus leaf and wrap a second time. Tuck in the loose ends; use cocktail sticks to secure if necessary.

6 On a well-floured surface, gently roll out the dough into a large rectangle about 1cm/½in thick. Put the leaf-wrapped chicken on top and bring up the dough to enclose the chicken completely. Pinch the seams well to seal and patch any holes with dough scraps.

7 Put the chicken in the roasting pan. Brush the dough with water and bake for 30 minutes, then reduce the heat to 180°C/350°F/Gas 4 and bake for 1½ hours longer, or until the dough is brown and dry. There may be small fissures and cracks. To serve, crack open the dough and carve the chicken at the table, then serve the chicken and stuffing with rice.

Cook's tip
The pastry and lotus leaves are not intended to be eaten, so parchment can be substituted for the lotus leaves, though you will lose the aroma the leaves provide.

Serves 4

1 small chicken, about 900g/2lb
15ml/1 tbsp Shaoxing wine
  or dry sherry
2.5ml/½ tsp salt
2 dried lotus leaves
boiled rice, to serve

For the dough wrapping
800g/1¾lb/7 cups plain (all-purpose)
  flour, plus extra for dusting
7ml/1½ tsp easy bake (rapid-rise)
  dried yeast
5ml/1 tsp sugar
5ml/1 tsp salt
450ml/¾ pint/scant 2 cups
  warm water
2 egg whites, lightly beaten

For the stuffing
4 dried shiitake mushrooms
90g/3½oz dried vegetable (mui choi)
30ml/2 tbsp vegetable oil
25g/1oz fresh root ginger,
  peeled and grated
4 garlic cloves, chopped
1 small onion, halved and
  thinly sliced
150g/5oz/generous ½ cup minced
  (ground) pork or chicken
½ small carrot, coarsely grated
2 spring onions (scallions), chopped
30ml/2 tbsp light soy sauce
15ml/1 tbsp Shaoxing wine
  or dry sherry
5ml/1 tsp sesame oil
2.5ml/½ tsp ground white pepper

Per portion Energy 305kcal/1284kJ; Protein 15g; Carbohydrate 44g, of which sugars 4g; Fat 8.5g, of which saturates 2g; Cholesterol 43mg; Calcium 104g; Fibre 4g; Sodium 363mg.

Rice wine chicken

Many cooking wines are made from rice, usually glutinous, and are generally termed bai jiu or mi chiu (white liquor). In Jiangxi Province, chefs are fond of steeping chicken and meats in wine overnight before they are cooked. The result is an intense alcoholic flavour, as most rice wines are 30 per cent proof. Start preparations the day before, if possible.

1 Trim off all excess fat from the chicken. Rub both the inside and outside with the salt. Mix the rice wine with the crushed garlic, sesame oil and pepper, and rub all over the chicken. Put the chicken in a sealable plastic bag, press out as much air as you can, then seal. Leave to marinate in the refrigerator for at least 4 hours or overnight. Turn the chicken every once in a while so that every part is evenly marinated.

2 When ready to cook, bruise the ginger with a pestle or a heavy rolling pin until it cracks but remains in one piece. Push the ginger and the spring onions, folded in half, into the chicken cavity.

3 Put the chicken on a deep plate that will fit into your steamer. Pour any remaining marinade over it. Steam over medium-high heat for 1 hour, or until very tender. Chop into portions and serve warm or cold.

Serves 4

1 chicken, about 1.2kg/2½lb
5ml/1 tsp salt
60ml/4 tbsp rice wine
15ml/1 tbsp crushed garlic
5ml/1 tsp sesame oil
2.5ml/½ tsp ground white pepper
large piece of fresh root ginger,
  the size of a plum, peeled
3 spring onions (scallions)

Cook's tip Served cold, this goes well with warmed Chinese rice wine or Japanese sake.

Per portion Energy 289kcal/1211kJ; Protein 40g; Carbohydrate 5g, of which sugars 2g; Fat 13g, of which saturates 3g; Cholesterol 159mg; Calcium 48g: Fibre 0g; Sodium 600mg.

Chicken and ginseng stew

Ginseng is a strange-looking root known the world over as an elixir. In China it has been revered for centuries and it has gained a reputation around the world as a super restorative. It can be worth its weight in gold but most Chinese herbal stores sell a range that is not too prohibitively expensive. It is a strong herb and you need only a few shreds to impart its intoxicating flavour (you don't actually eat the ginseng, as it has a fibrous texture). Its botanical name is Panax ginseng – the word panax meaning 'cure all' in Greek. Its wide-ranging curative properties are believed to include increasing muscle tone and stimulating the metabolism. Cloves are added to the dish to heighten the flavour and temper the bitterness of the ginseng.

1 Trim the chicken of all excess fat. Combine all the ingredients except the soy sauce and spring onions in a heavy pan and bring to the boil over medium heat. Reduce the heat, then cover and simmer gently for 1½ hours, or until the chicken is tender and falling off the bone.

2 Carefully transfer the chicken to a platter. Leave to cool slightly, then remove the bones and coarsely shred the meat. Strain the cooking liquid into a clean pan and add the chicken meat, then return to a gentle simmer over medium heat.

3 Serve hot, garnished with sliced spring onion and with a dish of dark soy sauce as a dip for the chicken.

Serves 4

1 chicken, about 1.2kg/2½lb
3 slices of ginseng root
40g/1½oz fresh root ginger, peeled
5ml/1 tsp salt
1.2 litres/2 pints/5 cups water
6 cloves
dark soy sauce, for dipping
finely sliced spring onions (scallions),
  to garnish

Cook's tip You can use ginseng granules instead of root, though they do not have the restorative properties.

Per portion Energy 260kcal/1090kJ; Protein 39g; Carbohydrate 1g, of which sugars 0g; Fat 11g, of which saturates 3g; Cholesterol 159mg; Calcium 33g; Fibre 0g; Sodium 597mg.

Prime Minister's chicken stew

History does not identify which prime minister this dish was in honour of, only that it is a banquet offering that no doubt pleased one Chinese Premier enough for it to go down in history. It is still common practice, especially in Taiwan, for chefs to prepare a particular dish for certain politicians. In ancient Shanghai, this dish was cooked to please an imperial Mandarin. It is a hearty stew containing chicken, pork and Chinese ham (Jinhua) braised in Chinese rice wine, and could grace any grand banquet today. If you cannot find Chinese ham, substitute with Spanish Serrano ham, or similar smoked varieties.

1 Cut the chicken into six to eight pieces. Cut the belly pork and ham joint into large chunks. Bring a large pan of water to the boil, add the ham and cook it for 10 minutes, then drain.

2 Heat the oil in a wok over medium-high heat. Fry the ginger slices, turning often, until lightly browned. Add the pork and stir-fry for 2 minutes.

3 Add the chicken, ham and all the other ingredients, except the quail's eggs and spring onions, to the wok. Bring to a simmer, then cover and braise for 45 minutes.

4 Check the meats for tenderness, and continue to simmer for a further 10–20 minutes, if necessary. The broth should be thick and rich-tasting. Meanwhile, boil the quail's eggs for 5 minutes. Drain and cool in cold water, then remove the shells.

5 Add the quail's eggs and spring onions to the wok, and simmer for 1 minute more. Serve hot, with boiled rice.

Serves 6–8

1 chicken, about 1.2kg/2½lb
165g/5½oz belly pork, without skin
250g/9oz smoked ham joint
30ml/2 tbsp vegetable oil
40g/1½oz fresh root ginger,
  peeled and sliced
5ml/1 tsp salt, or to taste
2.5ml/½ tsp sugar
2.5ml/½ tsp ground white pepper
800ml/27fl oz/scant 3¼ cups water
100ml/3½fl oz/scant ½ cup
  rice wine
12 quail's eggs
3 spring onions (scallions),
  cut into 5cm/2in lengths
boiled rice, to serve

Cook's tip Traditionally, duck eggs are included, but these can be difficult to find, so quail's eggs are used instead.

Per portion Energy 277kcal/1159kJ; Protein 34g; Carbohydrate 1g, of which sugars 1g; Fat 15g, of which saturates 5g; Cholesterol 438mg; Calcium 50g: Fibre 0g; Sodium 589mg.

Braised chicken with taros

Taro is a particular favourite of Fuzhou chefs, turning up in many dishes either mashed and wrapped or added as a starchy staple to stews and stir-fries. Taro is widely used across the world but its versatility is most manifest in Chinese cookery. Taros can be as large as papayas or as small as plums, their white flesh stippled with brown or purple. The small baby ones are particularly delicious in this dish. Look out for them in Chinese, Japanese or Caribbean supermarkets or grocers.

1 Steam the taros for 10 minutes over medium heat, until barely tender.

2 Trim the chicken of any excess fat, skin and gristle, and chop into bitesize pieces. Rinse with boiling water and drain thoroughly.

3 Heat the oil in a wok over high heat, add the garlic and fry for 20 seconds. Add the chicken pieces and stir-fry over high heat for 2 minutes, or until lightly browned.

4 Add the oyster sauce, sesame oil, pepper and salt, and stir for 30 seconds. Add 750ml/ 1¼ pints/3 cups water, then cover and simmer gently for 20 minutes.

5 Add the taro pieces and simmer, uncovered, for 5–8 minutes, or until the taros are tender and the sauce is thick.

6 Add the spring onions and cook for 30 seconds more. Serve hot with plain boiled rice or steamed bread.

Serves 4

3 taros, peeled and chopped
   into large chunks, or 6 baby
   taros, peeled and halved
1 chicken, about 1.2 kg/2½lb
15ml/1 tbsp vegetable oil
2 garlic cloves, crushed
30ml/2 tbsp oyster sauce
5ml/1 tsp sesame oil
2.5ml/½ tsp ground black pepper
2.5ml/½ tsp salt
3 spring onions (scallions), chopped
boiled rice or Chinese steamed
   bread, to serve

Per portion Energy 429kcal/1805kJ; Protein 41g; Carbohydrate 32g, of which sugars 2g; Fat 16g, of which saturates 4g; Cholesterol 159mg; Calcium 72g; Fibre 4g; Sodium 668mg.

Chicken in spring onion sauce

The wonderful flavour of this dish belies the simplicity of its cooking method. Shanghai chefs have the knack for transforming common, basic ingredients into ambrosial sauces, which exalt everyday chicken, meat or fish to the highest levels. For this dish, it is important to use chicken with the skin on, as the true texture and taste of the chicken rely on the alchemy of skin and meat.

1 Cut the chicken into slices about 2cm/³⁄₄in thick, each slice containing both meat and skin. Rub the chicken slices with rice wine, salt and pepper, and arrange them on a wide plate that will fit into your steamer.

2 Blanch the spring onions in simmering water for 5 seconds to soften.

3 Drape the spring onions and ginger strips over the chicken. Steam over medium-high heat for 10 minutes. Remove from the heat and leave the chicken in the steamer, tightly covered, for 10 minutes more.

4 To make the sauce, combine the cooked and sesame oils in a small pan and warm over medium heat until hot. Stir in all the other sauce ingredients, which should sizzle when added. Remove from the heat, stir the sauce well, and pour it over the chicken. Serve hot or cold.

Cook's tip Cooked oil is vegetable oil that has been brought to just under smoking point, then allowed to cool, or oil that has been previously used to fry items such as crispy shallots. It adds a slightly caramelized, nutty note to dishes.

Serves 4

4 chicken breast fillets, with skin
5ml/1 tsp rice wine
2.5ml/½ tsp salt
2.5ml/½ tsp ground white pepper
2 spring onions (scallions),
  cut into 10cm/4in lengths
4 thin slices of fresh root ginger,
  cut into strips

For the sauce
45ml/3 tbsp cooked oil
  (*see* Cook's Tip)
10ml/2 tsp sesame oil
2 spring onions (scallions),
  chopped finely
25g/1oz fresh root ginger, peeled
  and finely grated
3 garlic cloves, crushed
2.5ml/½ tsp salt

Per portion Energy 267kcal/1114kJ; Protein 30g; Carbohydrate 2g, of which sugars 1g; Fat 15g, of which saturates 2g; Cholesterol 88mg; Calcium 23g; Fibre 0g; Sodium 569mg.

Snow flower chicken

Like many Chinese recipe names, the origin of the name of this dish from Fujian province is a mystery, though there are many theories. According to the late Kenneth Lo, owner of the London restaurant Memories of China, one theory has it that when the chicken is steamed, the glutinous rice coating almost resembles snowflakes. Whatever the origins of the name, it is a very pretty dish that is also extremely tasty.

1 Mix together the soy sauce, sesame oil, pepper, rice wine and 45ml/3 tbsp water in a shallow bowl. Cut the chicken breast fillets into large cubes and marinate in the mixture for 20 minutes.

2 Drain the rice well and spread thinly over a large plate. Whisk the egg white and 15ml/1 tbsp water until frothy, then add the cornflour and beat well to make a light paste. Drain the chicken pieces from the marinade, reserving the marinade. Dip each piece in the paste to coat thoroughly, then roll in the glutinous rice until completely and evenly coated.

3 Arrange the chicken pieces in a single layer in a large, wide heatproof dish that will fit into your steamer, and steam over medium-high heat for 45 minutes. Put the marinade in a pan and bring to the boil over low heat. Simmer for several seconds, then pour over the steamed chicken before serving.

Serves 4–6

15ml/1 tbsp light soy sauce
5ml/1 tsp sesame oil
2.5ml/½ tsp ground white pepper
45ml/3 tbsp rice wine
4 chicken breast fillets, about 600g/1lb 5oz total weight
250g/9oz white glutinous rice, soaked overnight
1 egg white
30ml/2 tbsp cornflour (cornstarch)

Cook's tip Minced (ground) pork, shaped into balls, can also be cooked in the same way, in which case omit the water from the marinade and do not drain the marinated pork.

Per portion Energy 284kcal/1196kJ; Protein 27g; Carbohydrate 39g, of which sugars 0g; Fat 2g, of which saturates 0g; Cholesterol 70mg; Calcium 15g: Fibre 0g; Sodium 252mg.

Serves 4

3 dried chillies, soaked in water for
  20 minutes
30ml/2 tbsp vegetable oil
2 garlic cloves, chopped
450g/1lb boneless chicken breast
  fillet, cut into 2cm/¾in cubes
15ml/1 tbsp hoisin sauce
15ml/1 tbsp rice wine
15ml/1 tbsp yellow bean sauce
2.5ml/½ tsp sugar
5ml/1 tsp cornflour (cornstarch)
1 spring onion (scallion), chopped
boiled rice, to serve

Per portion Energy 207kcal/869kJ; Protein 28g;
Carbohydrate 4g, of which sugars 2g; Fat 9g,
of which saturates 1g; Cholesterol 79mg;
Calcium 15g: Fibre 0g; Sodium 320mg.

Stir-fried diced chicken

*This recipe comes from Jiangxi Province, which borders Fujian to the east.
Its cuisine borrows freely from that of this neighbour as well as from that of
Hunan Province, as they share a common border. This dish is an aromatic
union, marrying the subtle cuisine of Fujian, which rarely features chillies,
with the fiery flavours of Hunan styles. It is all at once hot, sweet and tart,
and utterly divine. Serve with plain rice.*

1 Seed the soaked chillies and cut them into 1cm/½in pieces. Heat the oil in a wok over
medium-high heat and fry the garlic for 20 seconds. Add the chillies and fry for 30 seconds,
taking care not to scorch them.

2 Add the chicken pieces and stir-fry vigorously for 2–3 minutes, or until they turn opaque.
Add the hoisin sauce, rice wine, yellow bean sauce and sugar, and stir well for 40 seconds.

3 Blend the cornflour with 105ml/7 tbsp water and add it to the pan. Stir until the sauce
bubbles, thickens and coats the chicken pieces. Toss in the spring onion and stir for
10 seconds. Serve immediately, with boiled rice.

Cook's tip For more fire, use 15ml/1 tbsp vegetable oil and 15ml/1 tbsp chilli oil instead of
purely vegetable oil. The dish will then take on a lovely red sheen.

Chicken with chestnuts

Chestnuts really come into their own in Chinese cooking; their rustic looks belie a husky sweetness and deliciously crumbly texture. Chinese stores sell them shelled and dried. They have to be soaked or boiled until soft, but the brown membrane can be fiddly to remove. You can use canned chestnuts, but these do not cook well as they tend to break up easily. In Shanghai cooking, a whole bird is the norm but most would find chicken breast fillets easier to deal with.

1 If using dried chestnuts, drain them and remove any pieces of brown membrane, using a pair of tweezers. Discard any chestnut that is brown or cracked. Place them in a pan and cover with water, then bring to the boil and simmer, partially covered, for 25 minutes, or until cooked through. Drain and set aside.

2 Heat the oil in a wok over high heat. Fry the garlic for 20 seconds, then add the mashed bean curd and fry for 15 seconds.

3 Add the sugar, soy sauce and pepper, and fry for 20 seconds, then add the chicken cubes. Stir-fry for 1–2 minutes, or until the chicken is almost cooked.

4 Blend the cornflour with 120ml/4fl oz/½ cup water.

5 Add the chestnuts to the wok, followed by the cornflour mixture, and cook for 1–2 minutes more, until the sauce bubbles and thickens. Serve with rice, garnished with Chinese celery leaves.

Serves 4

15 dried chestnuts, soaked overnight, or 15 peeled cooked chestnuts
30ml/2 tbsp vegetable oil
3 garlic cloves, crushed
30ml/2 tbsp preserved red bean curd (tofu ru), mashed with a fork until smooth
5ml/1 tsp sugar
15ml/1 tbsp light soy sauce
2.5ml/½ tsp ground white or black pepper
4 chicken breast fillets, cut into 2cm/¾in cubes
7.5ml/1½ tsp cornflour (cornstarch)
chopped Chinese celery leaves, to garnish
boiled rice, to serve

Per portion Energy 460kcal/1945kJ; Protein 33g; Carbohydrate 56g, of which sugars 12g; Fat 13g, of which saturates 2g; Cholesterol 88mg; Calcium 99g: Fibre 9g; Sodium 395mg.

Chicken with cloud ear mushrooms

This much-loved fungus – not quite a mushroom in the familiar visual sense – is ubiquitous throughout China and especially in Fujian province. It has a smoky and woody flavour, keeps its crunch even after simmering and is touted for its medicinal properties as a blood purifier. Its flavour complements succulent meats like pork and chicken. Sold in dried form it has an almost limitless shelf life, if kept in an airtight container.

1 Slice the chicken into thin strips. Soak the cloud ears in cold water for 20 minutes, or until they swell up and acquire a slippery texture. Using scissors, trim off and discard any hard woody parts from the cloud ears, then cut them into fine strips.

2 Heat the oil in a wok over high heat. Fry the garlic for 10 seconds, then add the chicken and cloud ears. Stir for 1 minute, then add 120ml/4fl oz/½ cup water.

3 Cook vigorously for 1 minute, then add the water chestnuts, oyster sauce, hoisin sauce, pepper and salt. Stir until there is just a hint of sauce left.

4 Add the spring onions and stir to mix, then serve, with noodles.

Cook's tip For a more complex dish, combine a selection of fungi, such as sliced fresh or soaked dried shiitake mushrooms, soaked white fungus (which are like cloud ear mushrooms but are white and frilly instead) or oyster mushrooms.

Serves 4

2 boneless chicken breast fillets, about 150g/5oz each
40g/1½oz cloud ear (wood ear) mushrooms
30ml/2 tbsp vegetable oil
2 garlic cloves, finely chopped
10 water chestnuts, drained and coarsely diced
15ml/1 tbsp oyster sauce
15ml/1 tbsp hoisin sauce
2.5ml/½ tsp ground black pepper
¼ tsp salt
3 spring onions (scallions), chopped
noodles, to serve

Per portion Energy 169kcal/710kJ; Protein 16g; Carbohydrate 8g, of which sugars 2g; Fat 8g, of which saturates 1g; Cholesterol 44mg; Calcium 22g; Fibre 1g; Sodium 478mg.

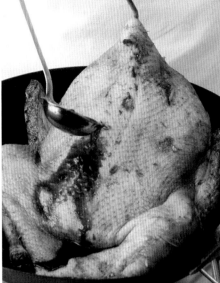

Marinated duck

With increasing tourism throughout eastern China, many visitors will no doubt fall in love with the incredible ambience and beauty of Zhejiang. Although one of China's smallest provinces, it is full of natural beauty, especially Hangzhou, which is known for its stunning topography, Dragon Well tea and exquisite cuisine. Purists would insist that the duck for this classic Zhejiang dish should be marinated and hung for two days, drained and re-marinated and then hung again for another two days – but this is a bit much for the home cook! As long as you marinate it overnight, the flavours will certainly impress your guests.

1 Rub the duck all over with salt and Chinese five-spice powder. Put it on a rack in a tray, and leave it in a cool place for 3–4 hours, or in the sun for 2 hours. Alternatively, chill it, uncovered, overnight. This will dry it out sufficiently.

2 Cut down either side of the backbone and remove it, then open the duck out like a spatchcock, pressing it down until flat. Rub both sides with wine or sherry and sugar, and sprinkle with chopped spring onions and ginger. Set aside for 1 hour in a cool place.

3 Bring the soy sauce to a simmer in a wok over low heat. Brush the flavourings off the duck back into the marinade and reserve, then pierce the duck neck with a metal S-hook. Hold the duck by the hook over the wok and ladle the sauce over the duck, until the skin is dark.

4 Place the duck in a deep heatproof dish that will fit in your steamer, and top with the spring onions and ginger from the marinade. Steam over high heat for 1½–2 hours, or until the meat is tender. Chop the duck into pieces and serve, garnished with spring onion, and with a dip.

Serves 4

1 oven-ready duck, about 2kg/
 4½lb in weight
2.5ml/½ tsp salt
1.5ml/¼ tsp Chinese five-spice
 powder
15ml/1 tbsp Shaoxing wine
 or dry sherry
5ml/1 tsp sugar
3 spring onions (scallions), chopped,
 plus extra to garnish
25g/1oz fresh root ginger, peeled
 and shredded
200ml/7fl oz/scant 1 cup light
 soy sauce
a sweet or spicy dip, to serve

Cook's tip For speed, use duck breasts, if you like, which are easier to cook and take half the time.

Per portion Energy 375kcal/1574kJ; Protein 51g; Carbohydrate 7g, of which sugars 6g; Fat 16g, of which saturates 5g; Cholesterol 275mg; Calcium 50g; Fibre 0g; Sodium 4083mg.

Meat

Cattle rearing was, and still is, relatively small-scale in China. The eating of beef is eschewed by many Taoists and Buddhists, and cows were traditionally treasured as beasts of burden – you can still see glimpses of rustic plough-pulling scenes in rural areas – so there is little beef on local menus. Pork is the universal meat of China even if eastern Chinese cuisine relies heavily on fish and shellfish. Whatever pork dish is served, it is the way it is cut that dictates the finished dish. Offal from pigs is given pride of place in the kitchen, and lamb and some game meats are also enjoyed.

Fragrant stir-fries and succulent ribs

The range of pork dishes from the eastern provinces is awe-inspiring. Each is given a special fillip with the appropriate seasonings and herbs, and is usually combined with vegetables and soya bean products, such as tofu and its pungent by-product sauces. Tofu in the form of preserved bean curd gives a tremendous lift to many an eastern Chinese meat dish. Pork in Preserved Bean Curd is a deeply satisfying dish when served with fluffy white rice.

Lychee Pork takes on a delicious sweet edge with the addition of these fragrant fruits. The Hangzhou dish of Tung-Po Pork has earned its global cachet as a dish that was inspired by a Song dynasty poet, Su Tung-Po. Today it is an eminent staple in Chinese restaurants around the world, as is Sweet-and-sour Spare Ribs, another eastern Chinese classic.

Belly pork is commonly used in China, but it is important to buy it with the correct ratio of lean meat to fat. A Chinese butcher will be able to provide you with a piece of meat that is suitable for your recipe. For quick-cooking stir-fries, lean pork tends to be used.

Lamb in Hot Bean Sauce or Stir-fried Kidneys with Ginger and Celery are more unusual offerings. In this region, offal is regarded with much respect, and these 'spare parts' are combined with local rice wine or one of the pungent sauces to create sumptuous results. The appearance of frog's legs on the menu here may seem curious, but they have, in fact, been used in Shanghai cuisine for hundreds of years.

Frog's legs in bean sauce

Most commonly associated with French cuisine, frog's legs have been a star item in Shanghai cooking for centuries. When properly cooked, they taste much like young chicken but have a milder flavour and a slightly chewy texture. The nutrients in frog meat have for a long time been deemed restorative and helpful in building young muscles, so they are a popular food for children. Farmed frogs are very common in the swamps and wetlands of eastern China. Frozen frog's legs are widely available in Chinese stores and are always sold skinned and cleaned as attached pairs.

1 Heat 45ml/3 tbsp oil in a wok over high heat. Fry the frog's legs a few at a time until partially cooked and lightly browned, about 3–4 minutes per batch. Add a little more oil to the wok if necessary. Drain the frog's legs on a rack as each batch is cooked.

2 Wipe out the wok and add 15ml/1 tbsp oil. Fry the ginger and garlic for 1 minute, until fragrant and browned, then add the yellow and black bean sauces, sugar, pepper and sesame oil, and stir to blend.

3 Add the frog's legs and stir-fry for 1 minute, being careful not to scorch them, then add 120ml/4fl oz/½ cup water and cook for several seconds more until the legs are thickly glazed with sauce. Serve hot, garnished with shredded spring onions or fresh coriander.

Serves 4

about 60ml/4 tbsp vegetable oil
16 pairs prepared frog's legs
30ml/2 tbsp thinly sliced fresh
    root ginger
3 garlic cloves, thinly sliced
15ml/1 tbsp yellow bean sauce
5ml/1 tsp black bean sauce
5ml/1 tsp sugar
2.5ml/½ tsp ground white pepper
5ml/1 tsp sesame oil
shredded spring onions (scallions) or
    fresh coriander (cilantro), to garnish

Cook's tip For a crisper finish, dust the frog's legs with cornflour (cornstarch) and deep-fry them until golden, instead of stir-frying them.

Per portion Energy 289kcal/1206kJ; Protein 28g; Carbohydrate 3g, of which sugars 2g; Fat 19g, of which saturates 3g; Cholesterol 105mg; Calcium 12g; Fibre 0g; Sodium 185mg.

Pork in preserved bean curd

Preserved bean curd comes in two forms: a peachy white type with a pungent sharpness, and a red type fermented with crushed red rice (a special rice inoculated with a red fungus), which has a heady aroma and an intense rosy hue. Both are potent seasonings. The red variety is preferred in the cuisine of eastern China, especially that of Shanghai. In Jiangxi province, pork is often cooked with preserved bean curd for a hearty dish to be eaten with rice.

1 Combine the pork with the bean curd and half the garlic, and leave to marinate, tightly covered, for at least 15 minutes. This will allow the pork to be fully steeped in flavour.

2 Heat the oil in a wok over high heat. Add the ginger and remaining garlic, and fry for 40 seconds until lightly browned. Add the pork with all its marinade and stir-fry for 2 minutes.

3 Add the sugar and leek, and fry for 1 minute, then add 200ml/7fl oz/scant 1 cup water. Bring to the boil and simmer for 2 minutes, or until the sauce is thick and the pork is cooked through. Serve piping hot, with rice or congee.

Serves 4

450g/1lb boneless pork shoulder,
  cut into 1cm/½in cubes
2 cubes red or white preserved bean
  curd (tofu ru)
3 garlic cloves, finely chopped
30ml/2 tbsp vegetable oil
15ml/1 tbsp shredded fresh
  root ginger
5ml/1 tsp sugar
1 leek, white part only, thinly sliced
boiled rice or congee, to serve

Variation Any kind of firm vegetables can be added to this dish, if you like. Celery and white radish, cut into matchsticks, are ideal.

Per portion Energy 224kcal/935kJ; Protein 25g; Carbohydrate 3g, of which sugars 2g; Fat 12g, of which saturates 3g; Cholesterol 71mg; Calcium 42g; Fibre 1g; Sodium 80mg.

Lychee pork

Nubby-skinned lychees are iconic Chinese fruits that have become popular all over the world. Sweet, succulent and dripping with juice, they are more than a dessert fruit and are put to good use in many stir-fried and sweet-and-sour dishes. Fresh lychees can usually only be bought in season, but canned lychees are universally available. Indigenous to sub-tropical China and Thailand, they can grow to the size of small plums. Interestingly, some restaurants offer a similarly named dish that does not actually contain the fruit but has the meat cut into floral shapes that resemble lychees. This dish, however, does contain this delicious fruit.

1 Tenderize the pork a little with the blunt edge of a cleaver or a meat mallet. Cut the slices into cubes, then dredge with cornflour and shake off the excess.

2 Heat the oil for deep-frying in a wok or deep-fryer over medium heat, and deep-fry the pork, in batches, until crisp and golden brown, about 2–3 minutes per batch. Drain on kitchen paper.

3 Combine 30ml/2 tbsp of the lychee juice with the vinegar, soy sauce, water, rice wine and salt. Heat the vegetable oil in a wok over high heat. Add the spring onions and fry for 20 seconds, then add the lychee sauce mixture and bring to the boil.

4 Add the pork and lychees, and stir-fry for 1 minute, or until the sauce is thick. Serve immediately with rice, and garnished with the reserved green parts of the spring onions, sliced in thin strips.

Serves 4

300g/11oz lean pork, cut into
  2.5cm/1in thick slices
50g/2oz/½ cup cornflour (cornstarch)
vegetable oil, for deep-frying
12 fresh or canned lychees, drained,
  pitted and halved, juice reserved
15ml/1 tbsp rice vinegar
15ml/1 tbsp light soy sauce
15ml/1 tbsp water
10ml/2 tsp rice wine
2.5ml/½ tsp salt
15ml/1 tbsp vegetable oil
2 spring onions (scallions),
  white parts only, chopped (reserve
  the green parts for the garnish)
boiled rice, to serve

Per portion Energy 267kcal/1118kJ; Protein 17g; Carbohydrate 19g, of which sugars 7g; Fat 14g, of which saturates 2g; Cholesterol 47mg; Calcium 18g: Fibre 1g; Sodium 573mg.

Pork with Chinese chives

Chinese chives are one of China's most favoured vegetables and are quite different from those used in Western cuisines, which tend to be served only as garnishes. Chives are found in three forms throughout China: flat, slim-bladed green chives, which are usually stir-fried or chopped to enliven fillings for dumplings and spring rolls; yellow chives, which are grown under cloches to keep them pale and silky; and a different vegetable altogether, the thick-stemmed flowering garlic chives, which are tipped with pointed green buds. Green or yellow chives are used here.

1 Cut the pork into thin matchsticks across the grain and combine with the rice wine, sesame oil, salt and pepper. Leave to marinate, covered, for 10 minutes.

2 Heat the vegetable oil in a wok over high heat. Stir-fry the garlic for 30 seconds until light brown. Add the pork with its marinade and fry for 1 minute, then add the chives and stir-fry vigorously for 1–2 minutes more, until the chives are deep green or yellow and just tender. Serve immediately with rice or Chinese steamed bread.

Variation This recipe is also delicious made with tender spring lamb.

Serves 4

250g/9oz lean pork
15ml/1 tbsp rice wine
5ml/1 tsp sesame oil
2.5ml/½ tsp salt
2.5ml/½ tsp ground white pepper
30ml/2 tbsp vegetable oil
2 garlic cloves, finely chopped
200g/7oz Chinese green or yellow
  chives, cut into 5cm/2in lengths
boiled rice or Chinese steamed
  bread, to serve

Per portion Energy 174kcal/725kJ; Protein 14g; Carbohydrate 4g, of which sugars 4g; Fat 11g, of which saturates 2g; Cholesterol 39mg; Calcium 75g; Fibre 1g; Sodium 296mg.

Serves 4

8 small dried shiitake mushrooms
400g/14oz lean pork, cut into strips
  5mm/¼in wide
10ml/2 tsp rice wine
2.5ml/½ tsp sugar
2.5ml/½ tsp ground white pepper
115g/4oz crisp white or green cabbage
30ml/2 tbsp vegetable oil
2 garlic cloves, sliced
30ml/2 tbsp dark soy sauce
shredded spring onions (scallions),
  to garnish

Per portion Energy 166kcal/697kJ; Protein 23g;
Carbohydrate 9g, of which sugars 2g; Fat 4g,
of which saturates 1g; Cholesterol 63mg;
Calcium 25g; Fibre 1g; Sodium 607mg.

Pork with cabbage and mushrooms

The stir-frying technique is used at all levels of Chinese cuisine, from rural home kitchens to imperial fine-dining restaurants. The goal is the same in every case, to bring out the very best flavour of the ingredients, using the precise and brief application of heat.

1 Soak the mushrooms in warm water for 1 hour, until softened. Strain and reserve the soaking water. Snip off and discard the mushroom stems and cut the caps into quarters.

2 Combine the pork with the wine, sugar and pepper in a bowl, and set aside. Shred the cabbage coarsely but evenly, and blanch in a pan of boiling water for 20 seconds. Drain well.

3 Heat the oil in a wok over high heat. Fry the garlic for 20 seconds, then add the pork and stir-fry for 1 minute. Add the mushrooms and cabbage, and fry for 1 minute more, then add the soy sauce and 150ml/¼ pint/⅔ cup of the reserved mushroom-soaking liquid. Stir for 1–2 minutes more, until the liquid has almost all evaporated. Serve immediately, garnished with shredded spring onions.

Variation The large white cabbage-like Chinese leaves (Chinese cabbage) can be used in place of cabbage if you prefer, as it has a similar taste. It will not need blanching, as it is tender and cooks quickly.

Tung-Po pork

A Hangzhou dish, this has a genuine pedigree, because Su Tung-Po, a famous poet and gourmet of the Song Dynasty (960–1279), actually lived in this city and was its governor for a few years. The dish has become popular all over the world, and is now a featured dish in many restaurants. Traditionally, belly pork is used, but if you deem this too fatty, use a leaner cut streaked with some fat. True Tung-Po pork always has the skin on. Traditionally, the belly pork skin is first browned in hot fat before the whole piece is boiled. This version omits the frying step.

1 Cut the belly pork into three or four large chunks. Bring a large pan of water to a simmer over medium-high heat, add the pork belly and blanch for 10 minutes. (This tenderizes and plumps up the pork.) Drain the pork and reserve the stock for use in another recipe.

2 Put the crushed sugar and wine in a deep heatproof dish that will fit into your steamer and lay the pork pieces on top. Drizzle evenly with soy sauce, and top with ginger and spring onions.

3 Put the dish in a steamer with a tight-fitting lid and steam over high heat for at least 1 hour, or until the pork is fork-tender. Uncover and baste the pork with the juices a few times during steaming.

4 Allow the pork to cool slightly, then slice it into thin pieces. Serve with the steaming juices poured over (strained, if you like), with plain rice and a side dish of stir-fried vegetables.

Variation Another version of this dish uses gammon (smoked or cured ham) or fresh bacon, which has to be soaked in cold water overnight and then drained and rinsed before boiling. This will create a saltier dish.

Serves 4

400g/14oz belly pork
40g/1½oz/scant ¼ cup rock or
  crystallized sugar, crushed
30ml/2 tbsp Shaoxing wine
  or dry sherry
30ml/2 tbsp soy sauce
25g/1oz fresh root ginger, peeled
  and shredded
4 spring onions (scallions) cut into
  5cm/2in lengths
boiled rice and stir-fried vegetables,
  to serve

Per portion Energy 307kcal/1282kJ; Protein 20g; Carbohydrate 13g, of which sugars 12g; Fat 20g, of which saturates 7g; Cholesterol 71mg; Calcium 24g: Fibre 0g; Sodium 600mg.

Stewed pork and vegetables

Chinese cooking does not begin and end with stir-fries. In temperate China, slowly-stewed dishes are often cooked and eaten to help ward off the chill of winter. This particular dish comes from Hangzhou, where it can get quite cold during the winter months, and is much loved as warming sustenance. Dried cole vegetables – sturdy-leaved members of the brassica family that resemble pak choi (bok choy) when fresh and olive-green rags when dried – are most often used in this Hangzhou dish. Lily buds, always sold dried, are a common ingredient.

1 Remove the skin from the belly pork and reserve for another dish or discard. Cut the meat into 2.5cm/1in cubes. Soak the dried vegetables or lily buds in tepid water for 20 minutes, or until softened. Cut off and discard any hard tips or roots, then wash and drain, and cut the vegetables into short lengths.

2 Heat the oil in a wok or flameproof casserole over medium-high heat until very hot. Add the garlic and fry for 20 seconds. Add the pork and fry for 2 minutes, until lightly browned.

3 Add the soy sauce, sugar and 750ml/1¼ pints/3 cups water and bring to the boil. Add the dried vegetables or lily buds and cover the pan, leaving the lid a little ajar. Adjust the heat to maintain a gentle simmer. Cook for 1–1¼ hours, until the pork is meltingly tender.

4 Stir in sesame oil and salt to taste, and serve piping hot, garnished with spring onions and accompanied by congee or rice.

Variation You can also add other dried ingredients such as soaked dried scallops and dried oysters to the pan, which will make for a much more intensely savoury dish.

Serves 4

400g/14oz belly pork
75g/3oz dried cole vegetables or
   dried lily buds
30ml/2 tbsp vegetable oil
3 garlic cloves, halved
45ml/3 tbsp light soy sauce
5ml/1 tsp sugar
5ml/1 tsp sesame oil
salt
chopped spring onions (scallions),
   to garnish
congee or boiled rice, to serve

Per portion Energy 326kcal/1357kJ; Protein 23g; Carbohydrate 10g, of which sugars 9g; Fat 22g, of which saturates 8g; Cholesterol 71mg; Calcium 97g: Fibre 5g; Sodium 879mg.

Fuzhou pork

A blindingly crimson paste made from the lees of red rice wine seasons many Fuzhou meat and poultry dishes. Although it is occasionally sold in Chinese stores, it is usually very difficult to find outside of China. Instead, I have suggested using the more common, similarly flavoured fermented red bean curd, which is coloured with red yeast rice. This is the kind of dish that takes pride of place when guests are invited to dinner.

1 Remove the skin from the belly pork. Cut into strips and cut each strip into bitesize pieces.

2 Combine the pork and taro in a wide heatproof dish that will fit into your steamer, and steam over hot water at high heat for 15 minutes.

3 Heat the oil in a wok over high heat. Stir-fry the garlic for 20 seconds, then add the preserved bean curd and stir-fry for 15 seconds, making sure that it does not scorch. Add the hoisin sauce and sugar, and stir for 15 seconds more.

4 Add the steamed pork and taro, and stir-fry vigorously for 1 minute. Add 120ml/4fl oz/ 1/2 cup water, stir well and cover. Reduce the heat to medium and cook for 1 minute, then uncover and cook for 1 minute more. Add the spring onions and mix well, then serve immediately with rice or Chinese steamed bread, garnished with sliced spring onion.

Serves 4

350g/12oz belly pork
150g/5oz taro, peeled and cut into
  2.5cm/1in cubes
15ml/1 tbsp vegetable oil
3 garlic cloves, finely chopped
25ml/1½ tbsp mashed preserved red
  bean curd (tofu ru)
15ml/1 tbsp hoisin sauce
2.5ml/½ tsp sugar
2 spring onions (scallions), chopped
sliced spring onion, to garnish
boiled rice or Chinese steamed
  bread, to serve

Cook's tip If you can find red rice wine lees, use 15ml/1 tbsp in place of the bean curd, and add it to the wok with the hoisin sauce and sugar.

Per portion Energy 320kcal/1335kJ; Protein 18g; Carbohydrate 14g, of which sugars 4g; Fat 22g, of which saturates 7g; Cholesterol 62mg; Calcium 42g: Fibre 1g; Sodium 218mg.

Pork chops in brown sauce

The eponymous brown sauce has nothing to do with the British table sauce, but is merely a description of its colour. It is a typical Fuzhou blend of soy sauce, oyster sauce, wine, pepper and the aromatics garlic, onion and cloves. This dish has crossed borders and been copied by Cantonese chefs, but it is really a Fuzhou classic. The recipe uses pork chops, which are not traditionally used in Chinese cooking. Normally, a rib cut would be used, but chops are universally available and work well in this dish. Seek out chops that have a thin rind of fat, as it will impart flavour.

1 Sandwich the pork chops between sheets of clear film (plastic wrap) and beat with a meat mallet until they are about 5mm/¼in thick. Dip the flattened chops in beaten egg to coat lightly, then dredge with cornflour.

2 Heat the oil for deep-frying over medium heat. Deep-fry the chops until golden brown, then drain briefly on kitchen paper and set aside.

3 Whisk all the sauce ingredients together to blend. Heat the oil in a clean wok over high heat and fry the garlic for 30 seconds, until golden brown. Add the onion and cloves and fry for 1–2 minutes more, until softened but not browned.

4 Add the sauce mixture and bring to the boil. Cook for 2 minutes or until reduced by about half, then add the cornflour mixture and stir for 30 seconds more, until the sauce bubbles and thickens.

5 Slice each pork chop into three to four pieces, then add to the sauce and toss well. Serve immediately, with steamed pak choi, if you like.

Serves 4

4 boneless pork chops, about
  175g/6oz each
1 egg, lightly beaten
50g/2oz/½ cup cornflour
  (cornstarch), plus 5ml/1 tsp
  blended with 15ml/1 tbsp water
vegetable oil, for deep-frying
15ml/1 tbsp vegetable oil
2 garlic cloves, finely chopped
1 large onion, halved and sliced
4 cloves
steamed pak choi (bok choy),
  to serve (optional)

For the sauce
300ml/½ pint/1¼ cups water
30ml/2 tbsp dark soy sauce
15ml/1 tbsp oyster sauce
15ml/1 tbsp Shaoxing wine
  or dry sherry
2.5ml/½ tsp ground black pepper

Per portion Energy 443kcal/1850kJ; Protein 39g;
Carbohydrate 18g, of which sugars 4g; Fat 24g,
of which saturates 6g; Cholesterol 172mg;
Calcium 41g: Fibre 1g; Sodium 839mg.

Sweet-and-sour spare ribs

So typically Chinese, you would inevitably come across sweet-and-sour dishes in whichever Chinese province you happen to be dining. They may not always be named as such, even though they have the famous blend of sweet and sour flavours. You can use a number of sweetening agents, including plum sauce, honey, sugar and pineapple juice, and you can adjust the amount of sweetening to taste. Vinegar or lemon juice provides the unique sour balance. Plum sauce, pineapple and rice vinegar provide the contrasting tastes in this dish.

1 Toss the ribs in beaten egg, then dredge with cornflour and shake off the excess.

2 Heat the oil for deep-frying in a wok or deep-fryer and deep-fry the pork ribs until deep golden brown; 2–3 minutes per batch. Remove them with a slotted spoon and drain them well on kitchen paper.

3 Combine the tomatoes, pineapple, plum sauce, pineapple juice, soy sauce, vinegar and water in a wok. Bring to the boil over medium heat, stirring constantly.

4 Add the pork ribs and stir until well blended and the pork is glossy with sauce. Serve immediately, with finger bowls, if you like.

Cook's tip Making sweet-and-sour sauce should hold no mystery. Do note, however, that a little bit of a salty element – the soy sauce – is necessary to keep the sweet and sour tastes in balance, or else the contrast may become too sharp.

Serves 4

600g/1lb 5oz pork ribs, chopped into 5cm/2in pieces (ask your butcher to do this for you)
1 egg, lightly beaten
40g/1½oz/⅓ cup cornflour (cornstarch)
vegetable oil, for deep-frying
2 small tomatoes, cut into six wedges each
10 pineapple chunks
30ml/2 tbsp plum sauce
15ml/1 tbsp pineapple juice
15ml/1 tbsp light soy sauce
15ml/1 tbsp rice vinegar
125ml/4fl oz/½ cup water

Per portion Energy 386kcal/1612kJ; Protein 25g; Carbohydrate 19g, of which sugars 10g; Fat 24g, of which saturates 7g; Cholesterol 137mg; Calcium 31g: Fibre 1g; Sodium 374mg.

Salt and pepper spare ribs

This Fujian dish is a regular part of family meals, especially on festive occasions, and is particularly tasty when made with really thick, meaty ribs. When cooked with salt and pepper, as here, pork ribs are ambrosial. When buying ribs, the weight of the bones means that you may need to buy more than you think. Restaurants sometimes deep-fry this dish, but the ribs can become greasy and overcooked. This version is stir-fried.

1 Blanch the pork ribs in a large pan of simmering water for 20 minutes. Lift them from the pan with a large mesh strainer. While they are still warm, dust them all over with cornflour, patting it on to help it to adhere.

2 Bring the pan of water back to a simmer and blanch the ribs for 45 seconds, then transfer to a plate.

3 Heat the groundnut and sesame oils in a wok over high heat. Add the ginger and fry for 15 seconds.

4 Add the ribs, salt, sugar and pepper, and stir-fry vigorously for 2–3 minutes, or until the ribs are lightly browned. For a moister texture, drizzle a tablespoon or two of the cooking liquid into the wok as you fry. Serve the ribs piping hot, garnished with Chinese celery leaves.

Variation Crushed Sichuan peppercorns can be used instead of, or in combination with, black peppercorns, for a more pungent flavour.

Serves 4

800g/1³/₄lb meaty pork ribs, chopped into 7.5cm/3in lengths (ask your butcher to do it for you)
30ml/2 tbsp cornflour (cornstarch)
15ml/1 tbsp groundnut (peanut) oil
10ml/2 tsp sesame oil
15ml/1 tbsp finely grated fresh root ginger
5ml/1 tsp salt
5ml/1 tsp sugar
5ml/1 tsp ground black or white pepper
Chinese celery leaves, to garnish

Cook's tips The ribs' cooked cornflour coating helps the seasonings to cling on to the meat.

Per portion Energy 383kcal/1595kJ; Protein 29g; Carbohydrate 9g, of which sugars 1g; Fat 26g, of which saturates 8g; Cholesterol 106mg; Calcium 14g: Fibre 0g; Sodium 594mg.

Lion's head pork balls

This noble-sounding Shanghai dish is every bit as grand-tasting as its name implies. The lion reference is simply because the minced pork dumplings are supposed to look vaguely like a lion's head, with the Chinese leaves representing the mane. This is a famous dish throughout eastern China, most particularly in Shanghai. The ratio of fat to lean meat is important for flavour and succulence, so use a cut of leg meat that is marbled with some fat.

1 Cut the pork into very thin slices, then into very thin strips. With a repetitive chopping motion, mince (grind) the pork on a chopping board using a heavy knife or cleaver for about 1 minute; halfway through, scrape up the pork into a ball and spread it out again. The minced (ground) pork should not be completely smooth, but should hold together well.

2 Scrape the minced pork into a bowl, and add the spring onion, ginger, wine or sherry, soy sauce, iced water, sesame oil, sugar, water chestnuts and 15ml/1 tbsp of the cornflour. Stir in one direction until the mixture clings loosely together. Shape the mixture into balls the size of small plums, and dust lightly with the remaining cornflour.

3 Bring the stock to a gentle boil in a pan. Gently lower the meatballs into the pan; they should be spread out in a single layer. Turn the heat to very low, cover and cook for 45 minutes. The liquid should barely bubble.

4 Heat the oil in a clean pan over high heat. Fry the Chinese leaves for 30 seconds, until softened. Carefully scoop the meatballs out of their pan and place on top of the Chinese leaves. Bring the meatball-cooking liquid to a full boil over high heat, then gently pour over the meatballs and leaves.

5 Reduce the heat and simmer the meatballs and leaves gently for 20 minutes more. Ladle into a serving dish, making sure the 'lion's heads' are on top. Serve immediately.

Serves 4

450g/1lb slightly fatty pork
  leg meat, well chilled
1 spring onion (scallion),
  finely chopped
15ml/1 tbsp finely grated fresh
  root ginger
30ml/2 tbsp Shaoxing wine
  or dry sherry
15ml/1 tbsp light soy sauce
15ml/1 tbsp iced water
5ml/1 tsp sesame oil
2.5ml/½ tsp sugar
6 water chestnuts, fresh if possible,
  peeled and finely diced
45ml/3 tbsp cornflour (cornstarch)
600ml/1 pint/2½ cups light pork
  or chicken stock
15ml/1 tbsp vegetable oil
200g/7oz Chinese leaves (Chinese
  cabbage), cut into 5cm/2in pieces

Per portion Energy 300kcal/1256kJ; Protein 23g; Carbohydrate 14g, of which sugars 3g; Fat 16g, of which saturates 5g; Cholesterol 74mg; Calcium 47g: Fibre 1g; Sodium 600mg.

Lamb in hot bean sauce

When the Shanghai winter chill begins to bite, citizens turn to hearty meats and sizzling dishes to warm them. Lamb is especially warming when cooked in a rich blend of bean sauce and chillies, wine and aromatics. Better still, serve it on a preheated cast-iron hot plate like those used in Chinese restaurants, to give an attractive talking point. Chinese stores sell these cast-iron plates, which you simply heat over a gas flame or in the oven and then place on a wooden base for safe handling.

1 Slice the lamb thinly with a cleaver, and tenderize it by beating with the cleaver's blunt edge or using a meat mallet. Cut the slices across the grain into very thin strips. Mix the lamb strips with the wine or sherry, salt and garlic paste, then cover and leave to marinate for 10 minutes.

2 Heat the vegetable and sesame oils in a wok over high heat. Fry the ginger for 1 minute, or until browned, then add the chilli bean paste and sugar, and stir for 30 seconds, being careful not to scorch the paste.

3 Add the lamb and its marinade, and stir-fry for 1 minute. Add the spring onions and pepper, and stir-fry for 1 minute more.

4 Add 100ml/3½fl oz/scant ½ cup water and cook vigorously until the juices become a thick sauce glazing the ingredients. Transfer to a hot plate (see Cook's Tip) or warmed serving bowls, and garnish with chopped spring onions. Serve with rice.

Cook's tip The best way to serve the lamb is on a hot plate, which creates an appealing sizzle when the lamb is put on to it. It also maintains the piping-hot serving temperature.

Serves 4

450g/1lb lean lamb or best end
  of neck fillet
30ml/2 tbsp Shaoxing wine
  or dry sherry
2.5ml/½ tsp salt
15ml/1 tbsp garlic paste
30ml/2 tbsp vegetable oil
15ml/1 tbsp sesame oil
25g/1oz fresh root ginger,
  peeled and shredded
30ml/2 tbsp chilli bean paste
  (dou banjiang)
2.5ml/½ tsp sugar
2 spring onions (scallions),
  cut into 5cm/2in lengths
1 red or green (bell) pepper,
  halved, cored and thinly sliced
chopped spring onions, to garnish
boiled rice, to serve

Per portion Energy 377kcal/1566kJ; Protein 23g; Carbohydrate 6g, of which sugars 6g; Fat 28g, of which saturates 9g; Cholesterol 84mg; Calcium 19g; Fibre 1g; Sodium 585mg.

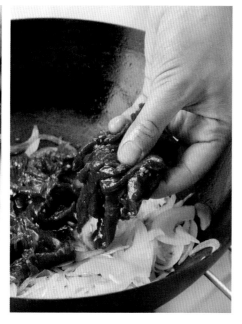

Shredded beef with celery

In Chinese cuisine, shredded beef requires a piece of sirloin or loin to be first sliced and then shredded with a sharp knife, or even a fine-edged metal spoon or ladle. This method yields exceptionally tender beef, which can then be used for quick stir-frying over high heat. Fillet will be even better for a sumptuous melt-in-the-mouth texture, if you are cooking for a special occasion.

1 Cut the beef into thin slices then, using a sharp knife, cut the slices across with a half-cutting, half-scraping motion to make thin julienne strips; they will be fragile.

2 In a bowl, mix together the soy sauce, rice wine, oyster sauce, pepper and 15ml/1 tbsp of the oil. Add the beef and gently mix to coat. Cover and leave to marinate in the refrigerator for 15 minutes.

3 Cut the celery sticks into 2cm/³⁄₄in pieces and then chop some of the celery leaves to make about 30ml/2 tbsp.

4 Heat the remaining oil in a wok over high heat. Fry the onion, stirring constantly, for 2 minutes or until softened and lightly browned.

5 Push to one side of the wok and add the beef and its marinade. Stir-fry for 1 minute, then mix the onion into the beef and fry for 30 seconds more. Add the celery sticks and leaves, and fry for a further 15 seconds. Sprinkle with sesame seeds and serve immediately, with rice.

Cook's tip This dish does not wait around for anybody – serve it immediately or the freshness of its flavours will dissipate.

Serves 4

450g/1lb beef sirloin, loin or
 fillet (tenderloin)
15ml/1 tbsp light soy sauce
15ml/1 tbsp rice wine
10ml/2 tsp oyster sauce
2.5ml/¹⁄₂ tsp ground white pepper
45ml/3 tbsp vegetable oil
150g/5oz Chinese celery sticks,
 with leaves
1 large onion, halved and
 thinly sliced
10ml/2 tsp lightly toasted sesame
 seeds, to garnish
boiled rice, to serve

Per portion Energy 302kcal/1258kJ; Protein 28g; Carbohydrate 7g, of which sugars 5g; Fat 18g, of which saturates 4g; Cholesterol 57mg; Calcium 60g: Fibre 2g; Sodium 475mg.

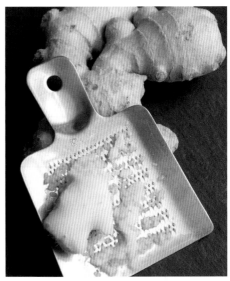

Stir-fried kidneys with ginger and celery

In China, offal meats (innards) are not regarded as secondary to main meats, and are thus accorded a status rarely granted to them in the West. The skilled cooking of liver, kidneys, tripe and brain can reach great culinary heights. This dish hails from Fujian and would have formed part of an imperial banquet. Mei kuei lu chiew – literally 'rose essence liquor' – is derived from kaoliang wine made in north China from sorghum and millet, by distilling it with rock sugar and a particular species of rose.

1 Halve the kidneys and open them out, then remove the white core from all halves. Rinse very well, pat dry with kitchen paper, then soak the kidney halves in fresh cold water for 30 minutes.

2 Cut each kidney half into three or four pieces. With a sharp knife, make deep cross cuts on the outer side, but only halfway through. (When cooked, the kidneys will shrink slightly, making each piece curl and exposing the cross cuts that will look like short studs. The finer and closer the cross cuts, the more the studs resemble the fat petals of an opened flower.)

3 Rinse the kidney pieces again, pat dry on kitchen paper and combine with the wine and salt in a bowl. Cover and leave to marinate for 10 minutes.

4 Cut the celery sticks on the diagonal into 1cm/½in pieces. Roughly chop a few of the celery leaves. Heat the oil in a wok over high heat. Fry the ginger and garlic for 20 seconds, then add the kidney pieces with their marinade, and the celery sticks. Fry vigorously for 40 seconds. The kidneys will curl up and shrink a little.

5 Add the sesame oil, sugar and the cornflour mixture, and fry for 20 seconds more. Add the celery leaves, stir once and serve immediately.

Serves 4

2 pig's kidneys
30ml/2 tbsp rose-flavoured wine
  (mei kuei lu chiew) or dry sherry
2.5ml/½ tsp salt
2 Chinese celery sticks, with leaves
30ml/2 tbsp vegetable oil
25g/1oz fresh root ginger, peeled
  and shredded
3 garlic cloves, finely chopped
10ml/2 tsp sesame oil
2.5ml/½ tsp sugar
5ml/1 tsp cornflour (cornstarch),
  blended with 30ml/2 tbsp water

Cook's tip Rose wine is relatively expensive, but its alluring fragrance makes all the difference to this dish. If you cannot find it, use the best-quality sherry you can get.

Per portion Energy 219kcal/910kJ; Protein 17g; Carbohydrate 3g, of which sugars 1g; Fat 14g, of which saturates 3g; Cholesterol 490mg; Calcium 18g: Fibre 0g; Sodium 270mg.

Rice and noodles

The Yangtze River delta provides the perfect environment for growing rice, and few Chinese, even in the far north where the grain does not grow, would sit down to a meal without the staple. Modern transportation has made it easily available even for remote communities, whether as rice on its own or a rice product such as rice flour, from which myriad noodles are made. Noodles are revered in eastern China and they come in endless varieties. Infinitely versatile, noodles inspire culinary inventiveness.

Hearty fillers and iconic dishes

The Yangtze River delta is a lush rice-growing landscape that produces some of the world's best grains. These range from fragrant jasmine rice to sticky glutinous rice from which comes not only rice wine but also rice noodles. Although wheat noodles are sometimes eaten here, it is rice and rice noodles that forms the basis of most meals. Boiled or steamed rice is served several times a day, often in the form of fried rice dishes, such as the glorious Yangzhou Fried Rice or the Shanghai classic, Fried Rice with Mixed Meats.

Rural families often prefer gruel-like porridge, such as Fish and Salt Egg Congee, and glutinous or sticky rice is a favourite staple among the rural communities due to the sustaining nature of its starchy content.

Shanghai's Jia Jiang Noodles, with the rich flavours of minced pork, rice wine, garlic, ginger and yellow bean paste, has become nothing less than iconic. Whether eaten for its symbolism, or satisfying sustenance, it is a real Shanghai classic.

A special variety of extremely fine rice noodles, which originated in Fujian but are now used throughout the region, are called mee sua. They are put to use in the quintessential Shanghai dish, Liver and Kidney in Fine Noodles. They are used on special occasions and can be recognized by the red string that holds the delicate bundles together. Mee sua may be difficult to find outside of China, so you can substitute other fine rice noodles instead.

Fish and salt egg congee

A real comfort food, congee is of peasant origin and is eaten in practically every province, city, town and family. This dish is the kind of supper congee that needs no accompaniments, and it is a favourite in Suzhou and throughout the eastern provinces. The fish used could be any type, but the best are the thick-filleted varieties such as cod, halibut, monkfish and salmon. It is the salted egg that gives the dish its special flavour.

1 Bring the rice and 1.5 litres/2½ pints/6¼ cups water to the boil in a large, heavy-based pan. Reduce the heat to maintain a slow simmer, then partially cover and cook for 30 minutes, stirring occasionally. Depending on the type of rice, you may have to top up the pan with more hot water if the congee thickens too quickly; it needs to become like a smooth porridge.

2 Slice the fish on a diagonal into 5mm/¼in thick slices, or alternatively into 2.5cm/1in cubes, removing any bones. Toss the fish with half the pepper and half the sesame oil, and set aside.

3 Boil the salted eggs over medium heat for 10 minutes, drain and rinse well with cold water. Shell and cut each egg into four to six pieces.

4 When the congee is soft and smooth, add the fish. Cook gently for another 3–4 minutes, or until the fish is just cooked through.

5 Add the egg pieces, soy or fish sauce and the remaining pepper and sesame oil, and lightly stir through. Serve immediately, topped with preserved vegetable, ginger and coriander.

Serves 4

150g/5oz/¾ cup jasmine rice, washed and drained (*see* Cook's Tip)
275g/10oz meaty fish fillet, such as cod, halibut, monkfish or salmon
5ml/1 tsp ground white pepper
10ml/2 tsp sesame oil
2 salted duck eggs
30ml/2 tbsp light soy sauce or fish sauce
15ml/1 tbsp preserved winter vegetable, shredded; fresh root ginger, peeled and sliced; and coriander (cilantro), to garnish

Cook's tip Traditionally, a broken medium-grain rice is used, which breaks down and releases starch to yield a smooth-textured porridge. You can simulate this by breaking up some of the raw rice with a mortar and pestle. Alternatively, replace 20g/¾oz of the rice with a short-grain variety, such as arborio.

Per portion Energy 223kcal/944kJ; Protein 14g; Carbohydrate 33g, of which sugars 1g; Fat 5g, of which saturates 1g; Cholesterol 35mg; Calcium 29g: Fibre 1g; Sodium 651mg.

Fried rice with beansprouts

The appearance of beansprouts in fried rice is a Hangzhou speciality, the vegetable being normally stir-fried and served as it is. The beansprouts are crunchy and thus provide a lively contrast to the rice, as well as the ham, which is also a main ingredient in this dish. Jinhua ham is on the dry side so, to make it more succulent, you can slice it thinly then blanch it for a minute or so in boiling water.

1 Your cooked rice should be completely cold. If it is in clumps, rake it through with a large fork to separate the grains. Heat the oil in a wok over high heat. Fry the spring onions for 45 seconds, or until softened and fragrant, then add the ham and stir for 20 seconds. Add the rice and stir-fry vigorously for 1 minute.

2 Add the oyster sauce, soy sauce and pepper, and stir for 30 seconds more, then add the beansprouts and fry for 1–2 minutes, or until they are crisp but tender. Serve immediately.

Serves 4

450g/1lb cold, cooked rice (225g/
  8oz/generous 1 cup raw weight)
30ml/2 tbsp vegetable oil
2 spring onions (scallions), chopped
185g/6$^{1}/_{2}$oz Jinhua ham, diced
  (*see* Cook's Tip)
15ml/1 tbsp oyster sauce
15ml/1 tbsp light soy sauce
2.5ml/$^{1}/_{2}$ tsp ground black pepper
90g/3$^{1}/_{2}$oz beansprouts

Cook's tip Jinhua ham is dry-cured and has an intense flavour. If this is unavailable, use any dry-cured ham.

Per portion Energy 300kcal/1260kJ; Protein 12g; Carbohydrate 37g, of which sugars 1g; Fat 13g, of which saturates 2g; Cholesterol 11mg; Calcium 37g: Fibre 3g; Sodium 833mg.

Yangzhou fried rice

As iconic as they come, this recipe for fried rice was born in the town of Yangzhou on the Yangtze River delta but has been so copied, especially by Cantonese restaurateurs, that its origin is often forgotten. It is sometimes advertised as Yang Chao Fried Rice, and is actually more high profile in Chinese restaurants overseas. In its home town it is no more than family staple fare, but the ingredients are classic, ranging from roast pork to prawns, eggs and peas, and sometimes ham and mushrooms. It is lovely served with pickled green chillies.

1 The cooked rice should be completely cold. If it is in clumps, rake it through with a large fork to separate the grains. Heat the oil in a wok over high heat. Add the garlic and fry for 20 seconds, then push it to one side of the wok and add the eggs. Break up the yolks and then scramble the eggs until half-set. Chop the eggs roughly with the wok ladle.

2 Add the rice, roast pork, prawns, soy sauce, pepper and salt, and stir-fry for 2–3 minutes. Stir vigorously with a to-and-fro motion, scraping the wok base and sides, so that all the ingredients are tossed and mixed well and the rice is thoroughly heated through.

3 Add the peas and spring onions and stir for 45 seconds. Serve immediately with pickled green chillies on the side.

Cook's tip The texture of Yangzhou Fried Rice is intended to be slightly grainy and this is best achieved if you use basmati or jasmine rice.

Serves 4

450g/1lb cold, cooked basmati or jasmine rice (225g/8oz/generous 1 cup raw weight)
30ml/2 tbsp groundnut (peanut) oil
3 garlic cloves, crushed and finely chopped
2 eggs
150g/5oz roast pork (cha shao), cut into 5mm/¼in dice
12 large prawns (shrimp), peeled and deveined
15ml/1 tbsp light soy sauce
4ml/¾ tsp ground white pepper
2.5ml/½ tsp salt, or to taste
30g/1¼oz/generous ¼ cup peas, thawed if frozen
2 spring onions (scallions), chopped
pickled green chillies, to serve

Per portion Energy 326kcal/1369kJ; Protein 19g; Carbohydrate 37g, of which sugars 1g; Fat 13g, of which saturates 3g; Cholesterol 238mg; Calcium 98g; Fibre 2g; Sodium 431mg.

Fried rice with mixed meats

Egg fried rice is very popular in Chinese restaurants outside China, but you will not find it anywhere in China. If rice is to be fried, it will always be enriched with a selection of meat, seafood or vegetables. Given that the dish evolved from the need to recycle leftover cooked rice, you can add anything you want to it. In Shanghai, fried rice is a complete meal in itself, and restaurant versions are studded with choice ingredients like prawns (shrimp), scallops, lobster or chicken.

1 Your cooked rice should be completely cold. If it is clumpy, rake it through with a large fork to separate the grains. Combine the Chinese sausages with 200ml/7fl oz/scant 1 cup water in a small pan and simmer over medium heat for 2 minutes, or until slightly softened. (Alternatively, sauté them in a few drops of oil.) Drain on kitchen paper.

2 Heat the oil in a wok over high heat. Fry the chopped onion for 1 minute, until softened, then push it to one side of the wok and add the eggs. Break up the yolks and then scramble the eggs until half-set. Chop the eggs roughly with the wok ladle.

3 Add all the remaining ingredients except the rice and peas and stir for 30 seconds. Add the rice and stir vigorously with a to-and-fro motion, scraping the wok base and sides, so that all the ingredients are tossed and mixed thoroughly. When the rice is fully heated through, add the peas and stir for 30 seconds. Serve immediately.

Cook's tips
• Never keep rice warm once cooked, as bacteria can develop. If you are going to keep it for using later, as in this recipe, cool it quickly by spreading it out on a plate, then chill it before use.
• If you are cooking rice specifically for later use in fried rice, use a meat or vegetable stock for part or all of the cooking water. This will enrich the dish and you will not need to add the oyster sauce.

Serves 4

450g/1lb cold, cooked rice
(225g/8oz/generous 1 cup raw
weight) (*see* Cook's Tips)
2 Chinese sausages, thinly sliced
30ml/2 tbsp vegetable oil
1 onion, finely chopped
3 eggs
75g/3oz/$^1/_2$ cup finely diced
cooked ham
75g/3oz/generous $^1/_2$ cup finely
diced cooked chicken
30ml/2 tbsp light soy sauce
15ml/1 tbsp oyster sauce
2.5ml/$^1/_2$ tsp ground white pepper
2.5ml/$^1/_2$ tsp sesame oil
25g/1oz/$^1/_4$ cup peas, thawed
if frozen

Per portion Energy 434kcal/1821kJ; Protein 22g;
Carbohydrate 40g, of which sugars 3g; Fat 22g,
of which saturates 5g; Cholesterol 209mg;
Calcium 65g; Fibre 2g; Sodium 1078mg.

Taoist vegetarian rice noodles

On certain days during the Lunar New Year celebrations (which actually last for two weeks), Taoist temples are packed with devotees praying to their ancestors and the different deities within the Taoist pantheon. Temple priests stir up huge woks of vegetarian noodles on the third day of the Lunar New Year, as this is deemed a universal vegetarian day. Bean curd wafers are thin brown pieces of dried tofu, about 7.5 x 5cm/3 x 2in.

1 Soak the shiitake mushrooms in warm water for 1 hour, until softened. Strain and reserve the soaking water and top it up to make 300ml/½ pint/1¼ cups. Snip off and discard the mushroom stems and slice the caps thinly.

2 Soak the dried lily buds in tepid water for 20 minutes, or until softened, then drain well. Snip off any hard tips. Wipe the bean curd wafers with a clean damp cloth. Cut them into 1cm/½in wide strips with kitchen scissors.

3 Heat the oil for deep-frying in a wok over medium heat or in a deep-fryer, and deep-fry the beancurd wafers until crisp. Drain on kitchen paper and set aside.

4 Soak the vermicelli in hot water for about 20 minutes or until they are soft and not brittle. Drain thoroughly and drizzle a little oil all over to prevent sticking.

5 Heat the oil in a wok over high heat. Add the garlic and fry for 20 seconds, until fragrant, then add the sliced mushrooms and lily buds. Fry for 1 minute, then add the Chinese leaves and fry 1 minute more.

6 Add the vermicelli, and stir-fry for 1 minute, then add two-thirds of the reserved mushroom liquor, the soy sauce and salt. Fry vigorously until the noodles are tender, sprinkling over the remaining mushroom water if they get too dry before they are cooked. Serve, sprinkled with fried bean curd wafer strips.

Serves 4

12 dried shiitake mushrooms
40g/1½oz dried lily buds
6 pieces sweet bean curd wafers
vegetable oil, for deep-frying
200g/7oz rice vermicelli
30ml/2 tbsp vegetable oil,
  plus extra for drizzling
3 garlic cloves, finely chopped
175g/6oz Chinese leaves
  (Chinese cabbage), sliced thinly
15ml/1 tbsp dark soy sauce
2.5ml/½ tsp salt, or to taste

Cook's tip This is not an overly seasoned dish and is intended to be rather bland. Within Taoist vegetarian beliefs, even eggs are not supposed to be used. If you do not need to be so strict, make a thin omelette from 2 or 3 eggs, cut into strips, and use them as a garnish.

Per portion Energy 417kcal/1713kJ; Protein 8g; Carbohydrate 5g, of which sugars 2g; Fat 20g, of which saturates 2g; Cholesterol 0mg; Calcium 113g; Fibre 3g; Sodium 521mg.

Dumpling noodles

Soupy noodles with wonton dumplings make a very satisfying breakfast or lunch choice. This Cantonese-style dish probably came by way of Hong Kong, where it is a street-food item. Fujian chefs will enrich their wontons with crab meat for a more robust flavour. As a soupy noodle dish, it is a complete meal in itself. You can use a light pork, chicken or fish stock: a traditional one is made with dried anchovies (known as ikan bilis in South-east Asia).

1 Combine the prawns, crab meat, soy sauce, cornflour, sesame oil and pepper, and mix thoroughly, stirring in one direction to compact the filling.

2 Take 1 heaped teaspoon of filling and wrap in a wonton skin. Run a wet finger around the rim of the skin, fold in half and press the edges well to seal, making a half-moon-shaped dumpling. Repeat with the remaining filling.

3 Bring a pan of water to a gentle but steady boil over medium-high heat. Simmer the dumplings for 2 minutes, or until cooked through, then drain and set aside on a plate.

4 Bring the stock to the boil and add the soy sauce and Chinese leaves. Simmer for 1 minute.

5 Blanch or boil the noodles according to the packet instructions, then drain. Divide the noodles and dumplings between the serving bowls, and ladle the hot stock and vegetables over. Garnish with pepper, spring onions and coriander leaves, and serve immediately.

Cook's tip Never cook dumplings directly in soup broth, as they will make it murky. Always cook them separately in boiling water and drain well before adding them to the soup.

Serves 4

100g/3¾oz prawns (shrimp), minced (ground)
100g/3¾oz white crab meat, minced (ground)
15ml/1 tbsp light soy sauce
5ml/1 tsp cornflour (cornstarch)
5ml/1 tsp sesame oil
2.5ml/½ tsp ground white pepper
16–20 round wonton wrappers
1.2 litres/2 pints/5 cups light stock
15ml/1 tbsp light soy sauce
115g/4oz Chinese leaves
  (Chinese cabbage), sliced into
  1cm/½in pieces
200g/7oz dry wheat noodles
ground white pepper, chopped spring
  onions (scallions) and coriander
  (cilantro) leaves, to garnish

Per portion Energy 285kcal/1208kJ; Protein 17g; Carbohydrate 46g, of which sugars 2g; Fat 5g, of which saturates 1g; Cholesterol 67mg; Calcium 49g: Fibre 4g; Sodium 847mg.

Braised noodles

When noodles are braised, it simply means that they are cooked slowly over a low heat. This treatment is usually reserved for a type of noodle called yi mien or yi fu. These are quite fine egg noodles, shaped like angel-hair pasta or thin linguine, but characterized by a golden colour. They have a slightly chewy texture due to the soda water used in making the dough. This simple dish from Fuzhou includes dried shrimps and onions. As dried shrimps are richly flavoured, the only seasoning needed is light soy sauce and a little pepper.

1 Drain and mince (grind) the shrimps finely with a cleaver or heavy knife.

2 Blanch the noodles in a large pan of simmering water until half-cooked; they should be flexible but firm to the bite. (Cooking times vary, so it is best to check the packet instructions and judge by tasting rather than timing.) Drain the noodles thoroughly and set aside.

3 Heat the oil in a wok over high heat. Add the onion and stir-fry for 1 minute, until softened and lightly golden.

4 Add the dried shrimps, soy sauce and water or stock, and bring to the boil. Add the noodles and simmer for 2–3 minutes, or until they are just tender, have absorbed most of the stock, and the remaining liquid has become a lightly thickened gravy. Season with pepper and salt and serve immediately, garnished with coriander or Chinese celery leaves.

Serves 4

130g/4½oz dried shrimps, soaked
  in hot water for 15 minutes
200g/7oz yi fu egg noodles
30ml/2 tbsp vegetable oil
1 large onion, quartered and
  thinly sliced
30ml/2 tbsp light soy sauce
550ml/18fl oz/2½ cups water or light
  chicken stock
4ml/¾ tsp ground white pepper
2.5ml/½ tsp salt, or to taste
chopped coriander (cilantro) or
  Chinese celery leaves, to garnish

Per portion Energy 367kcal/1545kJ; Protein 25g;
Carbohydrate 41g, of which sugars 4g; Fat 13g,
of which saturates 2g; Cholesterol 179mg;
Calcium 421g; Fibre 3g; Sodium 1703mg.

Serves 4

200g/7oz dry wheat noodles
5ml/1 tsp sesame oil
150g/5oz lean pork
10ml/2 tsp rice wine
10ml/2 tsp cornflour (cornstarch)
5ml/1 tsp light soy sauce
15ml/1 tbsp vegetable oil
2 garlic cloves, finely chopped
2.5ml/½ tsp ground white pepper
90g/3½oz pak choi (bok choy),
  thinly sliced
2 shredded spring onions (scallions),
  to garnish

Cook's tip Stir-fried noodles are often cooked with a minimal amount of liquid. The finished dish should not be awash with stock but have just enough to moisten the noodles.

Per portion Energy 283kcal/1196kJ; Protein 15g; Carbohydrate 42g, of which sugars 3g; Fat 8g, of which saturates 1g; Cholesterol 24mg; Calcium 35g; Fibre 3g; Sodium 124mg.

Hangzhou pork noodles

There are not enough words to do justice to the beauty of Hangzhou today, with its famous West Lake. Marco Polo was said to have likened Hangzhou to Venice, and some claim he took Hangzhou noodles west, though Italian culinary academics refute this. Dry wheat noodles come in many brands, but choose one that is close to spaghetti in thickness. Follow the packet instructions on how to re-hydrate them.

1 Cook the noodles in boiling water according to the packet instructions, and drain well. Toss the noodles in the sesame oil until thoroughly coated, then cover and set aside.

2 Slice the pork into thin matchsticks, then mix with the rice wine, cornflour and soy sauce. Set aside to marinate for 10 minutes.

3 Heat the vegetable oil in a wok over medium-high heat. Add the garlic and fry for 20 seconds, then add the pork and fry for 1 minute.

4 Add the pepper and 90ml/6 tbsp water, and stir-fry for 1 minute more.

5 Add the noodles and pak choi to the wok. Stir-fry vigorously for 1–2 minutes until the vegetables are crisp-tender and the noodles are heated through. Serve immediately, garnished with shredded spring onions.

Jia Jiang noodles

Although the spiritual home of this dish is Beijing, it was so popular that it crossed many borders over the centuries and is today as much a part of the eastern regional cooking school as the northern one. It is particularly entrenched in Shanghai; in fact some locals even claim that it originated here and was taken to the north when dynastic rulers combed the country for top chefs and the best dishes. Whatever its evolution, it is delicious.

1 Mix the minced pork with the rice wine, soy sauce, cornflour and sugar, then cover and set aside to marinate for 15 minutes.

2 Slice the cucumber into fine julienne strips. Cut the spring onions on a sharp diagonal into similarly thin strips. Set aside, covered with dampened kitchen paper so that the juliennes keep their crispness.

3 Heat the oil in a wok over high heat. Add the onion, garlic and ginger, and fry vigorously for 45 seconds–1 minute, or until fragrant. Add the yellow bean paste and fry for 20 seconds, then add the pork and stir-fry for 2 minutes.

4 Add 200ml/7fl oz/1 cup water and cook for 1 minute more, or until the liquid thickens into a light sauce. Season with salt to taste.

5 Cook the noodles in boiling water according to the packet instructions. Drain well and divide between serving bowls. Reheat the sauce if necessary and pour it over the noodles. Arrange the sliced spring onions and cucumber in small mounds next to the noodles and serve immediately.

Serves 4

225g/8oz/1 cup minced (ground) pork
30ml/2 tbsp rice wine
30ml/2 tbsp light soy sauce
15ml/1 tbsp cornflour (cornstarch)
5ml/1 tsp sugar
1 cucumber, peeled and cored
4 spring onions (scallions)
30ml/2 tbsp vegetable oil
½ large onion, finely chopped
3 garlic cloves, finely chopped
25g/1oz fresh root ginger, shredded
15ml/1 tbsp yellow bean paste
200g/7oz dry wheat noodles
salt

Cook's tip In other regions lamb or beef would be used instead of pork, but the vegetables remain the same.

Per portion Energy 355kcal/1495kJ; Protein 20g; Carbohydrate 49g, of which sugars 7g; Fat 10g, of which saturates 1g; Cholesterol 36mg; Calcium 60g: Fibre 4g; Sodium 678mg.

Liver and kidney in fine noodles

Rites of passage and birthdays are invariably celebrated with the serving of noodles (mien) to symbolize longevity. This quintessential Shanghai dish is a favourite for such celebrations. The noodles used are always a special variety: fine, almost bone-white, and extremely delicate. These are normally sold in boxes containing skeins of the noodles, each wrapped with a red string and intended for special occasions. They are believed to have originated in Fujian and are called mee sua in the dialect. If these are not available, use the thinnest rice or wheat noodles you can find.

1 Wash the pig's liver and pat it dry with kitchen paper. Slice it thinly. Halve the kidney and open it out, then remove the white core from both halves. Rinse well, pat dry, then slice the kidney thinly. Combine the liver, kidney and wine or sherry, and leave to marinate, covered, for 10 minutes.

2 Put the water in a large pan and return to a gentle simmer. Add the minced pork, stirring to break it up. Cook for 4–5 minutes.

3 While the pork is cooking, heat the sesame oil in a small pan over low heat and fry the garlic for 20 seconds. Add to the pork stock with the soy sauce.

4 Add the liver and kidney with their marinade, and cook for 1–2 minutes on high heat until the liver is just tender.

5 Immediately before serving, gently lower the noodles into the pan and cook for barely 1 minute, until just tender. Ladle the broth, noodles and liver and kidney slices into individual serving bowls, garnish with celery leaves and pepper, and serve immediately.

Serves 4

200g/7oz pig's liver
1 whole pig's kidney
30ml/2 tbsp Shaoxing wine or
  dry sherry
1 litre/1¾ pints/4 cups boiling water
100g/3¾oz/scant ½ cup minced
  (ground) pork
15ml/1 tbsp sesame oil
2 garlic cloves, finely crushed
30ml/2 tbsp light soy sauce
225g/8oz mee sua noodles
chopped Chinese celery leaves and
  5ml/1 tsp ground white pepper,
  to garnish

Cook's tip Unlike more robust noodles, mee sua do not need to be soaked or cooked separately, as they are so fine. Do not overcook them; they turn mushy very quickly.

Per portion Energy 368kcal/1541kJ; Protein 27g; Carbohydrate 45g, of which sugars 1g; Fat 8g, of which saturates 2g; Cholesterol 310mg; Calcium 23g; Fibre 3g; Sodium 675mg.

Vegetable dishes

Throughout China, vegetables are present in just about every meal, turning up either on their own as stir-fries or combined with meat, seafood and poultry in complex dishes. They are rarely served cold, because such dishes are generally not regarded as conducive to good health. Vegetables are cooked only to the point at which their nutrients are preserved. Stir-fried vegetables are important in eastern Chinese cuisine and, with the region producing a wide range of vegetables, the variety of dishes is endless.

Fresh, crunchy and nutritious

Many vegetables are grown in China, especially around the fertile Yangtze delta, that rarely, if ever, make it out of the country. Most local people shop for vegetables on a daily basis due to the cultural insistence upon fresh produce. The simplest of ingredients, such as mangetouts (snow peas), baby corn, pak choi (bok choy), kai lan, mushrooms, spring onions (scallions) and bamboo shoots are tossed with aromatic seasonings to create many tasty dishes.

Mushrooms are extremely versatile, and this is put to excellent use in wok-fried recipes such as Jade Button Mushrooms, and Bamboo Shoots with Mushrooms, as well as wonderful parcels of shiitake mushrooms wrapped in delicate bean curd skins.

Tofu features prominently alongside vegetables, as it has a chameleon quality that allows it to blend beautifully with just about every green. Tofu can be added to any vegetable dish to add protein. Gluten products, such as the 'sausages' that appear in the recipe Bamboo Shoots with Sausages, can play a similar role to tofu.

The recipes in this chapter are not all vegetarian, though some certainly are. Be aware that oyster sauce is not a vegetarian product; if you are cooking a vegetable dish for vegetarians, you can substitute a mushroom-based version instead. Buddha's Vegetarian Stew is a simple and nourishing meat-free dish.

Most of the vegetables used here are readily available in supermarkets and Chinese stores.

Stir-fried mixed vegetables

As stir-fries go, this Fujian dish is a template, and you can improvise by adding anything from the entire spectrum of vegetables within Chinese cuisine. The only part that must remain sacrosanct is stir-frying over intense heat. This is easy enough to achieve, even with slow-heating electric ranges. The important thing is to heat up your wok to a sufficient intensity, whatever the heat source. The time it takes to stir-fry vegetables is measured in seconds. If you pre-blanch them, the actual stir-frying takes even less time. This dish is not suitable for vegetarians as it contains oyster sauce.

1 Heat the oil in a wok over high heat until smoking and fry the garlic for 30–40 seconds, or until pale gold. Toss in all the vegetables and stir-fry vigorously for 1 minute.

2 Add the oyster sauce and sesame oil, and stir for 30 seconds, or until the juices thicken slightly. (The salt in the oyster sauce will draw out some liquid from the vegetables but, if necessary, add a little water should you need more sauce.) Serve hot.

Variation If you like courgettes (zucchini) and bitter melon, you can also use these in the dish. Choose firm young specimens and blanch them briefly before stir-frying. This reduces the cooking time and preserves the colour and crunch of the vegetables.

Serves 4

30ml/2 tbsp vegetable oil
2 garlic cloves, finely chopped
12 baby corn, halved
12 mangetouts (snow peas)
2 celery sticks, thinly sliced
200g/7oz green vegetables, such as kai lan, pak choi (bok choy) or flowering cabbage (choy sum), cut into 5cm/2in lengths
30ml/2 tbsp oyster sauce
5ml/1 tsp sesame oil
100ml/3$\frac{1}{2}$fl oz/scant $\frac{1}{2}$ cup water (optional)

Per portion Energy 112kcal/465kJ; Protein 3g; Carbohydrate 5g, of which sugars 3g; Fat 9g, of which saturates 1g; Cholesterol 0mg; Calcium 46g; Fibre 3g; Sodium 342mg.

Stir-fried beans with spring onions

In Chinese cooking, although specific types of vegetables are used for their intrinsic taste and texture, there are also many dishes that are generic. This stir-fried bean dish could be made with any type of bean, so you could choose another variety, if you prefer. In almost all stir-fried dishes, such as this one from Shanghai, a blend of seasonings is used. It is rare to see a dish without aromatics, as individual flavours are not a part of the culinary heritage. The most popular are bean-based sauces, some with pepper or chillies and others with aromatics like garlic, ginger, leeks and spring onions. Sesame oil is also used often, and is much loved for its nutty fragrance. Use the thickest spring onions you can find for this recipe.

1 Blanch the beans in a pan of boiling water for 20 seconds, then drain, rinse with cold running water, and drain again. Heat the oil in a wok over high heat and fry the ginger for 20 seconds. Add the chilli bean paste and sugar, and fry for 20 seconds.

2 Add the beans, spring onions and sesame oil, and stir-fry vigorously for 1–2 minutes, then sprinkle in 100ml/3½fl oz/scant ½ cup water. Fry for 1 minute, or until the beans are just tender. Serve immediately.

Serves 4

300g/11oz runner (green) beans,
  cut diagonally into pieces
  1cm/½in wide
15ml/1 tbsp vegetable oil
5ml/1 tsp ginger paste
15ml/1 tbsp chilli bean paste
  (dou banjiang)
2.5ml/½ tsp sugar
5 fat spring onions (scallions),
  cut into 5cm/2in lengths
5ml/1 tsp sesame oil

Per portion Energy 72kcal/297kJ; Protein 2g;
Carbohydrate 5g, of which sugars 4g; Fat 5g,
of which saturates 1g; Cholesterol 0mg;
Calcium 49g; Fibre 3g; Sodium 2mg.

Jade button mushrooms

Within Chinese symbolism, there are endless references to acquiring wealth, wisdom and longevity – the three most desired objectives in the culture. For instance, noodles are eaten for the promise of longevity, and oranges because they are coloured gold, as in wealth. Wisdom? Well, it can only come with longevity! Green vegetables are often likened to jade, which symbolizes wealth. Colours, textures and shapes are important in Chinese culinary philosophy and every chef strives to achieve the maximum effect in each dish.

1 Blanch the mustard greens in a pan of boiling water for 20 seconds, then drain, rinse with cold running water, and drain again. (This helps to preserve their green colour.)

2 Heat the oil in a wok and fry the garlic for 20 seconds. Add the greens and mushrooms, and stir-fry over high heat for 2 minutes.

3 Add the soy sauce, pepper and wine or sherry, and stir for 1 minute.

4 Blend the cornflour with 150ml/¼ pint/⅔ cup water and add to the wok. Stir until the sauce bubbles and thickens, then season with salt to taste. When serving, arrange the mustard greens so that they are prominent, as they are the 'jade' of the recipe name.

Serves 4

200g/7oz mustard greens (sian chai), cut into 4cm/1½in squares
30ml/2 tbsp vegetable oil
2 garlic cloves, crushed
200g/7oz/3 cups fresh button (white) mushrooms, thinly sliced
200g/7oz/3 cups straw mushrooms
30ml/2 tbsp light soy sauce
2.5ml/½ tsp ground white pepper
30ml/2 tbsp Shaoxing wine or dry sherry
5ml/1 tsp cornflour (cornstarch)
salt

Cook's tip Any green vegetable – such as mangetouts (snow peas), broad (fava) beans and spinach – can symbolize jade and will taste as delicious.

Per portion Energy 111kcal/461kJ; Protein 3g; Carbohydrate 5g, of which sugars 3g; Fat 8g, of which saturates 1g; Cholesterol 0mg; Calcium 34g: Fibre 4g; Sodium 543mg.

Serves 4

16 dried shiitake mushrooms, soaked
 for 1 hour in hot water
15ml/1 tbsp dark soy sauce
5ml/1 tsp garlic paste
5ml/1 tsp ginger paste
2.5ml/½ tsp salt
2.5ml/½ tsp ground white pepper
2.5ml/½ tsp sugar
5ml/1 tsp cornflour (cornstarch)
1 or 2 sheets of bean curd skin
chilli and garlic sauce, to serve

Cook's tips These bean curd skin
parcels are sometimes brushed with
a little lightly thickened stock after
steaming, to give them a glossy, juicy
finish. They can also be deep-fried, if
they are first sealed with a cornflour
and water paste. Bean curd skin crisps
up almost immediately in hot oil.

Per portion Energy 33kcal/140kJ; Protein 3g;
Carbohydrate 3g, of which sugars 1g; Fat 1g,
of which saturates 0g; Cholesterol 0mg;
Calcium 70g; Fibre2g; Sodium 252mg.

Mushrooms with bean curd skin

*The shiitake mushrooms used in this recipe, known as black mushrooms,
are the premium variety with large fissures in their caps. These are called
'winter mushrooms' in Fujian Province, and are eaten for their symbolism of
longevity as well as for their rich, husky flavour and meaty texture. Bean curd
skins are factory-produced. The film that forms on top of boiling soya milk is
lifted off and dried flat to form wrinkly sheets. The kind used here are the
slightly glossy, translucent brown skins, rather than the opaque yellow-beige
skins. These have a superior texture and flavour to spring roll skins.*

1 Drain the shiitake mushrooms, snip off and discard the stems and slice the caps as thinly
as you can. Marinate the mushroom slices with the soy sauce, garlic, ginger, salt, pepper,
sugar and cornflour for 10 minutes.

2 Lay a sheet of bean curd skin on a flat surface and wipe over gently with a damp cloth.
(This is to prevent it from cracking and splitting.) Cut into pieces 13cm/5in square.

3 Put 15ml/1 tbsp of mushroom mixture on the edge of each square and roll up like a spring
roll, tucking in the sides to seal as you go.

4 Put the rolls on a flat plate that will fit inside your steamer, and steam for 10–15 minutes.
Serve with a chilli and garlic sauce.

Serves 4

300g/11oz canned bamboo shoots
30ml/2 tbsp vegetable oil
2 garlic cloves, crushed
2 spring onions (scallions),
    white part only, chopped
200g/7oz/3 cups straw
    mushrooms, halved
15ml/1 tbsp dark soy sauce
2.5ml/½ tsp sugar
5ml/1 tsp cornflour (cornstarch)
salt

Bamboo shoots with mushrooms

In summer when the weather is warm, many Chinese will resort to dishes that have cooling properties, as dictated by traditional Chinese herbalism. Every Chinese ingredient is deemed either yin or yang, the former associated with coolness and the latter with heat. Then again, it can also depend on the method of cooking, as a yin product can become yang if ingredients like pepper and chillies are added. It's a minefield of near-mystical theories, but suffice to know that when a dish tastes good, one is left with a feeling of equanimity. This recipe is believed to have cool, yin, properties.

1 Slice the bamboo shoots into thin strips. Heat the oil in a wok over high heat. Add the garlic and fry it for 30 seconds, then add the spring onions and fry for 30 seconds more.

2 Add the bamboo shoots and mushrooms, and stir for 2 minutes. Add the soy sauce and sugar, and stir over high heat for 2 minutes.

3 Blend the cornflour with 120ml/4fl oz/½ cup water and add it to the wok, stirring. When the sauce thickens, season with salt and serve immediately.

Variation This is a basic stir-fry to which a plethora of vegetables, such as leeks, spinach and water chestnuts, can be added to taste.

Per portion Energy 94kcal/388kJ; Protein 2g;
Carbohydrate 4g, of which sugars 2g; Fat 8g,
of which saturates 1g; Cholesterol 0mg;
Calcium 21g: Fibre 3g; Sodium 274mg.

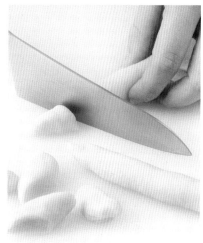

Bamboo shoots with sausages

This is a vegetarian dish, so it may seem surprising to find sausages in the title, but there is an explanation. Within the realm of Chinese vegetarian cooking there are many mock-meat products made chiefly from gluten. Some gluten products are so skilfully made that they actually look like chicken, duck, roast pork or sausage. These gluten sausages are now available in cans and vacuum packs in Chinese stores.

1 If you have bought your bamboo shoots as whole pieces, slice them into 1cm/½in thick pieces. If they are already sliced, leave them as they are. Soak in plenty of cold water for 20 minutes to reduce the canning brine. Drain thoroughly.

2 Drain the gluten sausages, or pieces, and gently squeeze out the excess moisture. Slice into pieces of similar size to the bamboo shoots.

3 Boil a large pan of water over high heat. Blanch the bamboo shoots for 20 seconds, then lift out with a slotted spoon and drain well. Blanch the gluten sausages for 1 minute and drain as before, then blanch the cabbage for 10 seconds and drain.

4 Heat the vegetable oil in a wok and fry the garlic until golden brown, then add the sesame oil, yellow bean sauce and sugar. Stir for 30 seconds, then add the blanched ingredients. Stir-fry for 1 minute. Add 120ml/4fl oz/½ cup water and bring to the boil. Simmer over high heat until only a small amount of liquid remains. Serve garnished with fried garlic or shallots.

Variation Firm or dried tofu cubes can be substituted for the gluten sausage. Rather than the normal soft tofu, these are fried cubes or squares that are sold in Chinese stores.

Serves 4

300g/11oz canned bamboo shoots
150g/5oz gluten sausages
  or other shapes
100g/3¾oz cabbage,
  cut into thin strips
30ml/2 tbsp vegetable oil
3 garlic cloves, crushed
15ml/1 tbsp sesame oil
30ml/2 tbsp yellow bean sauce
2.5ml/½ tsp sugar
crisp-fried garlic or shallots,
  to garnish

Per portion Energy 153kcal/631kJ; Protein 5g; Carbohydrate 3g, of which sugars 3g; Fat 13g, of which saturates 2g; Cholesterol 0mg; Calcium 221g: Fibre 2g; Sodium 194mg.

Tofu with preserved bean curd

Many vegetarian dishes in China feature tofu prominently, using the different types such as soft, firm, fried or pickled tofu, which all have a high protein content. In this recipe preserved bean curd seasons the sauce for two other kinds of bean curd or tofu. Typical of Hangzhou cooking, this dish is highly flavoured and on the salty side, and is intended to be eaten with congee. It is a comfort food from peasant origins. The two types of tofu used here are fried golden brown puffs, which have a slightly wrinkly skin, and a dried and almost pickled variety of tofu called tofu gan in Mandarin.

1 Soak the dried vegetable according to the packet instructions until it swells up. Rinse and drain, then cut into small pieces.

2 Heat the oil in a wok and fry the ginger for 45 seconds over medium heat. Add the mashed preserved red bean curd and stir-fry for 20 seconds.

3 Add both types of tofu, the sugar, sesame oil, wine or sherry and pepper. Stir for 1 minute and add 250ml/8fl oz/1 cup water. Braise for 20 minutes over medium heat until the barest hint of sauce is left. Serve garnished with celery leaves.

Serves 4

75g/3oz dried vegetable
  (see Cook's Tips)
15ml/1 tsp vegetable oil
25g/1oz fresh root ginger, pounded
  to a paste
1 cube preserved red bean curd
  (tofu ru), mashed until smooth
  with a fork
12 pieces of fried tofu puffs, halved
  (*see* Cook's Tips)
8 pieces of dried tofu wafers, halved
2.5ml/1/2 tsp sugar
15ml/1 tbsp sesame oil
30ml/2 tbsp Shaoxing wine
  or dry sherry
2.5ml/1/2 tsp ground black pepper
chopped fresh Chinese celery leaves,
  to garnish

Cook's tips

• When you buy dried vegetable it will be called Sichuan cai in Mandarin or mui choy in Cantonese.
• You can buy ready-fried tofu puffs, but if you cut firm fresh tofu into 2.5cm/1in cubes and deep-fry them slowly until golden, it will have a meatier texture.

Per portion Energy 187kcal/779kJ; Protein 9g; Carbohydrate 10g, of which sugars 8g; Fat 12g, of which saturates 1g; Cholesterol 0mg; Calcium 376g; Fibre 5g; Sodium 12mg.

Serves 4

30ml/2 tbsp vegetable oil
3 garlic cloves, chopped
3 eggs
150ml/¼ pint/⅔ cup unsweetened
    soya milk or full-fat (whole) milk
200ml/7fl oz/scant 1 cup light
    chicken or vegetable stock
a pinch of ground cloves
15ml/1 tbsp light soy sauce
2.5ml/½ tsp ground white pepper
4ml/¾ tsp salt
4 fresh shiitake mushrooms,
    very thinly sliced
1 spring onion (scallion), chopped

Per portion Energy 168kcal/696kJ; Protein 8g;
Carbohydrate 3g, of which sugars 2g; Fat 14g,
of which saturates 3g; Cholesterol 179mg;
Calcium 77g; Fibre 1g; Sodium 826mg.

Steamed eggs with mushrooms

This is a delicate dish cooked during the hot summer months in Shanghai when temperatures can be sweltering and appetites rendered sluggish. The lightness comes from the unusual addition of milk to the egg mixture. Traditionally, soya milk would be used, but cow's milk makes only a marginal difference to the taste. Unsweetened soya milk is widely available in UHT packs. If you want to make this dish for vegetarians, use vegetable stock.

1 Heat the oil in a small pan over medium-low heat and fry the garlic gently for 2 minutes, or until golden. Drain and set aside, reserving the oil. Lightly beat the eggs with the milk, stock, ground cloves, soy sauce, pepper and salt, then strain through a fine sieve (strainer) into a bowl.

2 Divide the sliced mushrooms between individual small heatproof bowls, or one large, shallow bowl, which will fit inside your steamer. Slowly pour in the eggs – it should not be more than 4cm/1½in deep.

3 Steam the eggs over gently simmering water for 25–30 minutes, or until the custard is only just softly set. Serve, garnished with fried garlic and oil, and chopped spring onion.

Cook's tip 10ml/2 tsp of chopped Chinese preserved vegetables (tung chai) can be added to this steamed dish for a smoky flavour. Chopped salted mustard greens (sian chai) will also give it a robust lift.

Oyster omelette

An iconic Fujian dish, this has been elevated to global status and is now a star item in many Chinese and South-east Asian restaurants overseas. Plump, good quality oysters should be used, but street food vendors, ever ingenious, will sometimes use the meat of other similar bivalves. The secret of the dish is in the use of water chestnut flour for the batter. Purists will insist on lard or white cooking fat as the cooking medium, but vegetable oil can be used instead, as here. The finished dish should be fully set but with juicy curds of egg, crispy shards of batter and barely cooked oysters.

1 Mix the water chestnut flour with 250ml/8fl oz/1 cup water to make a thin mixture, the consistency of milk. (If the flour feels very coarse, crush it with a mortar and pestle; however, a little grittiness is normal.)

2 Heat 15ml/1 tbsp of the oil over medium-high heat in a large frying pan (a wok is not suitable) until smoking hot. Pour in the flour mixture and swirl it to form a paper-thin crêpe. Cook until nearly set.

3 Add the eggs, one by one, and spread them around to cover the batter. Turn the heat up to high and fry until the batter is almost crisp, adding the remaining oil a little at a time during this process. This will make the batter very crisp.

4 Stir the flour and egg mixture for 1 minute to break it up and mix it together, then add the oysters. Stir for 30 seconds, then add the soy sauce, fish sauce, pepper, salt, spring onions and chilli sauce or paste, if using.

5 Stir for 30 seconds more, then serve immediately, garnished with fresh coriander.

Serves 4

60g/4 tbsp water chestnut flour
45ml/3 tbsp vegetable oil
6 eggs
12 large fresh oysters
15ml/1 tbsp light soy sauce
5ml/1 tsp fish sauce
2.5ml/½ tsp ground white pepper
¼ tsp salt
2 spring onions (scallions), chopped
15ml/1 tbsp hot chilli sauce
  or paste (optional)
chopped fresh coriander (cilantro),
  to garnish

Cook's tip If your heat is not high enough, the batter will turn gloopy instead of crisp. If you use a non-stick pan, only a scant amount of oil is needed to cook the batter.

Per portion Energy 140kcal/580kJ; Protein 5g; Carbohydrate 4g, of which sugars 2g; Fat 12g, of which saturates 1g; Cholesterol 21mg; Calcium 62g; Fibre 1g; Sodium 611mg.

Buddha's vegetarian stew

This is one dish rife with Buddhist symbolism. It originally used 18 different ingredients representing each one of the sage's disciples. The noble name for it is 18 Lohan, this being the Sanskrit name of the Buddha. Most families in China will cook a modified version of this dish, as it is very time-consuming to stir up 18 ingredients; however, you should have no fewer than half a dozen if the dish is going to taste any good. This is a truly glorious panful, a quintessential vegetarian dish that would surely please the Lord Buddha himself. It is traditionally prepared during the Lunar New Year and on festive occasions. It also keeps and freezes well.

1 Soak the shiitake mushrooms in warm water for 45 minutes, or until softened. Snip off and discard the stems, and slice the caps in half. Soak the cloud ear mushrooms in tepid water for 20–30 minutes, or until softened but not limp. Using scissors, trim off and discard any hard woody parts from the cloud ears and cut into large bitesize pieces.

2 Arrange all the ingredients in plates near to hand, as they have to be added to the wok in sequence. Heat the oil in a wok over medium heat and fry the garlic and ginger for 1–2 minutes, or until golden brown and fragrant. Add the preserved bean curd and yellow bean sauce to the wok. Stir-fry for 40 seconds, then add the hoisin sauce, sugar and salt, and fry for 20 seconds more.

3 Add the vegetables in this order, stirring for 10 seconds between additions: shiitake mushrooms, straw mushrooms, ginkgo nuts, lotus seeds, cloud ears, mangetouts and pak choi. Transfer the contents of the wok to a pan and add the sesame oil and 800ml/27fl oz/scant 3¼ cups water. Partially cover and simmer for 30 minutes until all the flavours are well blended.

Serves 4

8 large dried shiitake mushrooms
40g/1½oz dried cloud ear (wood ear) mushrooms
45ml/3 tbsp vegetable oil
6 garlic cloves, crushed to a paste
40g/1½oz fresh root ginger, grated
2 cubes preserved red bean curd, mashed till smooth with a fork
15ml/1 tbsp yellow bean sauce
30ml/2 tbsp hoisin sauce
5ml/1 tsp sugar
5ml/1 tsp salt
100g/3¾oz canned straw mushrooms, rinsed and drained
20 ginkgo nuts (vacuum-packed or canned), drained
20 lotus seeds (canned), drained
10 mangetouts (snow peas)
200g/7oz pak choi (bok choy), cut into 45cm/2 inch lengths
10ml/2 tsp sesame oil

Per portion Energy 224kcal/929kJ; Protein 7g; Carbohydrate 15g, of which sugars 5g; Fat 16g, of which saturates 2g; Cholesterol 0mg; Calcium 67g: Fibre 4g; Sodium 464mg.

Sweet things

It must be said that desserts do not really feature in typical Chinese meals. Sweet creations are generally intended as snacks, and are sold by itinerant street vendors or reserved for special festivals. Many are made with cooked pulses, like red beans or mung beans, sweetened with palm sugar or rock sugar. They may be an acquired taste for Western palates, but are certainly worth trying for their unusual, intense flavour.

Sweet soups and bean feasts

Wheat flour and butter rarely feature in Chinese desserts, but the range of sweet buns or dumplings can be extensive on special occasions. On festive days, anything sugary is symbolically regarded as a 'honeyed bribe' for departing deities on their way to their celestial homes.

Symbolism plays a large part in the sweet menu of eastern China. The dish Five-flavoured Soup is based on the theories of numerology, and is believed to treat the ills of the five vital organs of the human body.

The most common ingredients in the region's sweet dishes are: ginkgo nuts, lotus seeds, dates, sugared winter melon slices and sweet potatoes. These are all widely cultivated in eastern China and are relatively inexpensive locally. Today, even lotus seeds and ginkgo nuts are available in Chinese stores around the world.

Red beans play an important role in Shanghai's sweet dishes. They are often cooked, mashed and sweetened as a filling, but are also cooked with palm sugar in the typical dish Red Beans in Syrup. Mung beans are also great in desserts. In Fujian, they are simmered with sugar to make a porridge that is thickened with wheat flour.

The preferred sweetening agent in these provinces is rock sugar, with its large crystals that impart a subtle perfume along with its taste. Palm sugar is also common, and both of these types of sugar are available around the globe.

Five-flavoured soup

Not a soup in the Western sense, but a dessert. Numerology plays a significant role within traditional Chinese herbal preparations, and indeed within the culture. The idea of the correct balance between all parts of the human body – which includes the concepts of chi (body energy) and acupuncture – is based on the theory of the Five Elements: Water feeds vegetation to produce Wood that fuels Fire that produces ashes on Earth, which yields Metal. This same number is symbolic when applied to ingredients. Here, water and sugar do not count among the five.

Serves 4

50g/2oz dried longan meat

1 litre/1³/₄ pints/4 cups boiling water

8 pieces preserved sweet winter melon slices

100g/3³/₄oz/¹/₂ cup rock sugar

20 prepared (canned) lotus seeds, rinsed and drained

20 gingko nuts (vacuum packed or canned), rinsed and drained

20 Chinese red dates, pitted

1 Wash and soak the dried longan meat for 25 minutes to re-hydrate it, then drain.

2 Put the water in a large pan and return to the boil. Add the winter melon slices and half the rock sugar. Simmer for 10 minutes, or until the rock sugar has dissolved.

3 Add all the remaining ingredients and simmer for 10 minutes.

4 Taste for sweetness and add the remaining rock sugar if you find it is not sweet enough for your taste (longan meat and winter melon slices contain a fair amount of sugar already). Traditionally, this sweet soup is supposed to be very sweet.

Cook's tips

• It is time-consuming to prepare lotus seeds and ginkgo nuts from their dry state, as they require soaking for several hours, or even overnight, and then boiling for at least an hour to tenderize them. Canned or vacuum-packed versions are convenient and widely available in Chinese stores.

• Longan meat is bought in neat little blocks of the peeled and seeded fruit formed in tight clumps, and it can sometimes contain a little grit from the husks.

• Chinese red dates are usually sold with stones (pits) but these are easy to remove with a sharp knife.

Per portion Energy 409kcal/1741kJ; Protein 7g; Carbohydrate 96g, of which sugars 94g; Fat 2g, of which saturates 1g; Cholesterol 10mg; Calcium 72g: Fibre 8g; Sodium 54mg.

Serves 4

300g/11oz sweet potatoes
115g/4oz/generous ½ cup sugar
26 ginkgo nuts (vacuum-packed
  or canned), rinsed and drained
15ml/1 tbsp sweet potato
  flour (optional)

Cook's tips
• Ginkgo nuts are believed to be very
rich in restorative nutrients.
• You may also use canned lotus
seeds instead of ginkgo nuts.

Per portion Energy 193kcal/822kJ; Protein 1g;
Carbohydrate 49g, of which sugars 34g; Fat 0g,
of which saturates 0g; Cholesterol 0mg;
Calcium 21g: Fibre 2g; Sodium 71mg.

Sweet potatoes with ginkgo nuts

*Those from the eastern areas of China favour extraordinarily sweet dishes,
so many of their desserts, especially this one from Shanghai, are laden
with sugar. If you do not have a taste for such intensity, use less sugar,
as it will not alter the intrinsic taste too greatly. Sweet potato is already
naturally sweet. Look for varieties with orange or yellow flesh, as they
tend to have the best flavour for this dish.*

1 Cut the sweet potatoes into 1cm/½in thick slices and then into 5cm/2in squares. Bring
800ml/27fl oz/scant 3¼ cups water to the boil with the sugar and cook the sweet potatoes
for 10 minutes.

2 Add the ginkgo nuts and simmer for 5 minutes. Blend the sweet potato flour (if using) with
enough water to make a thin paste, and add to the pan. Stir until slightly thickened. If you
prefer to have a thin sauce, omit the sweet potato flour. Serve hot or cold.

Serves 4

300g/11oz/1¾ cups Chinese red
   beans or red kidney beans, soaked
   overnight, rinsed and drained
115g/4oz/½ cup palm sugar (jaggery)
800ml/27fl oz/scant 3¼ cups
   boiling water
2–3 pieces of tangerine peel

Cook's tip If palm sugar (jaggery)
is not available, use demerara (raw)
or muscovado (molasses) sugar.

Red beans in syrup

Kidney beans are a good option for this dish if you cannot get the smaller Chinese red beans, which are used locally. This recipe hails from Shanghai and is a peasant staple, dating back centuries. Traditionally, tangerine peel is added for a citrus tang. Like most pulses, red beans have to be soaked for several hours or overnight before use. They swell up considerably when soaked and cooked. Palm sugar is bought in small cylinders or, more recently, already liquefied and in bottles. If you use the solid type you will need to grate it into a small amount of water and then strain it.

1 Put the beans in a pan, add plenty of water and bring to the boil. Boil rapidly for 10 minutes, then cook for 30 minutes, or until very tender. Drain.

2 If using the solid palm sugar, grate with a sharp knife into a small pan with a little water and boil to dissolve the shavings. Once dissolved, strain the syrup through a fine sieve (strainer) to remove any grit.

3 Put the boiling water in a pan and add the beans, the strained, dissolved sugar, or the liquefied sugar, and tangerine peel. Simmer for 10 minutes, or until almost mushy. Serve either hot or warm.

Per portion Energy 305kcal/1299kJ; Protein 17g;
Carbohydrate 61g, of which sugars 28g; Fat 1g,
of which saturates 0g; Cholesterol 0mg;
Calcium 101g: Fibre 18g; Sodium 36mg.

Mung beans in syrup

As a late night snack or for breakfast, this sweet porridge is very popular among the Fujian people. Mung beans, from which you get beansprouts, have to be soaked overnight before they are soft enough to be simmered with brown sugar or palm sugar. There are two distinct versions of this dish – one using beans with the green skin still on, and the other with hulled beans in a thick sugar syrup. The recipe here is for the former version, which is popular in South-east Asia, having been introduced by the Chaozhou people from Shantou. Chinese stores sell both versions. Using more or less sugar is a matter of taste, and if palm sugar is not available, you can use demerara sugar instead. Taste and adjust accordingly as you add the sugar.

1 Put the boiling water in a large pan and return to the boil, then add the mung beans. Simmer for 15 minutes, then add the sugar. Continue to simmer until the mung beans are very soft and are almost breaking up.

2 Blend the sweet potato flour with enough water to make a slightly thickened liquid and add to the mung beans. Stir until thick. You may need to add more hot water if the mixture is too thick. (It should not be so thick that you see no liquid.) Serve warm.

Serves 4

1.2 litres/2 pints/5 cups boiling water
300g/11oz/1³⁄₄ cups mung beans,
  skin on, soaked overnight
  and drained
250g/9oz/1¹⁄₄ cups palm sugar
  (jaggery) or demerara (raw) sugar
50g/2oz/¹⁄₂ cup sweet potato flour

Per portion Energy 480kcal/2043kJ; Protein 19g; Carbohydrate 105g, of which sugars 57g; Fat 1g, of which saturates 0g; Cholesterol 0mg; Calcium 127g: Fibre 11g; Sodium 62mg.

Suppliers

UNITED STATES

The House of Rice Store
3221 North Hayden Road
Scottsdale, AZ 85251
Tel: (480) 947 6698

99 Ranch Market
140 West Valley Boulevard
San Gabriel, CA 91776
Tel: (626) 307 8899

Hong Kong Supermarket
18414 Colima Road
Los Angeles, CA 91748
Tel: (626) 964 1688

Seafood City Supermarket
1340, 3rd Avenue, Chula Vista
San Jose, CA 91911
Tel: (619) 422 7600

Ai Hoa
860 North Hill Street
Los Angeles, CA 90026
Tel: (213) 482 4824

Oriental Grocery
11827 Del Amo Boulevard
Cerritos, CA 90701
Tel: (310) 924 1029

Unimart American and
 Asian Groceries
1201 Howard Street
San Francisco, CA 94103
Tel: (415) 431 0326

Georgia Asian Foods, Etc.
1375 Prince Avenue
Atlanta, GA 30341
Tel: (404) 543 8624

Augusta Market Oriental Foods
2117 Martin Luther King
 Jr. Boulevard
Atlanta, GA 30901
Tel: (706) 722 4988

Hong Tan Oriental Food
2802 Capitol Street
Savannah, GA 31404
Tel: (404) 233 6698

Khanh Tan Oriental Market
4051 Buford Highway NE
Atlanta, GA 30345
Tel: (404) 728 0393

Norcross Oriental Market
6062 Norcross-Tucker Road
Chamblee, GA 30341
Tel: (770) 496 1656

The Oriental Pantry
423 Great Road
Acton, MA 01720
Tel: (978) 264 4576

May's American Oriental
 Market
422 West University Avenue
Saint Paul, MN 55103
Tel: (651) 293 1118

Nevada Asian Market
2513 Stewart Avenue
Las Vegas, NV 89101
Tel: (702) 387 3373

Dynasty Supermarket
68 Elizabeth Street
New York, NY 10013
Tel: (212) 966 4943

Asian Supermarket
109 E. Broadway
New York, NY 10002
Tel: (212) 227 3388

Kam Man Food
 Products
200 Canal Street
New York, NY 10013
Tel: (212) 571 0330

Hang Hing Lee Grocery
33 Catherine Street
New York, NY 10013
Tel: (212) 732 0387

Oriental Market
670 Central Park Avenue
Yonkers, NY 10013
Tel: (212) 349 1979

Asian Foods Ltd
260–280 West Leigh Avenue
Philadelphia, PA 19133
Tel: (215) 291 9500

Golden Foods
 Supermarket
9896 Bellaire Road
Houston, TX 77036
Tel: (713) 772 7882

Welcome Food Centre
9810 Bellaire Boulevard
Houston, TX 77030
Tel: (718) 270 7789

UNITED KINGDOM

Wing Yip
375 Nechells Park Road, Nechells
Birmingham, B7 5NT
Tel: 0121 327 3838

Sing Fat Chinese Supermarket
334 Bradford Street, Digbeth
Birmingham, B5 6ES
Tel: 0121 622 5888

Makkah Oriental Food Store
148–150 Charminster Road
Bournemouth, BH8 8YY
Tel: 01202 777303

Ryelight Chinese Supermarket
48 Preston Street
Brighton, BN1 2HP
Tel: 01273 734954

Wai Yee Hong
Eastgate Oriental City
Eastgate Road, Eastville
Bristol, BS5 6XY
Tel: 0845 873 3388

Wing Yip
544 Purley Way
Croydon, CR0 4NZ
Tel: 0208 688 4880

Hoo Hing Cash & Carry
Lockfield Avenue, Brimsdown
Enfield, EN3 7QE

Pat's Chung Ying Chinese
 Supermarket
199–201 Leith Walk
Edinburgh, EH6 8NX
Tel: 0131 554 0358

See Woo
Unit 5, The Point, 29 Saracen Street
Glasgow, G22 5H7
Tel: 0845 0788 818

Chung Ying Supermarket
254 Dobbies Loan
Glasgow, G4 0HS
Tel: 0141 333 0333

Rum Wong Supermarket
London Road
Guildford, GU1 2AF
Tel: 01483 451568

Seasoned Pioneers Ltd
101 Summers Road
Brunswick Business Park
Liverpool, L3 4BJ
Tel: 0151 709 9330

Loon Fung Supermarket
42–44 Gerrard Street
London, W1V 7LP
Tel: 0207 373 8305

New Loon Moon
 Supermarket
9a Gerrard Street
London, W1D 5PP
Tel: 0207 734 3887

Golden Gale Grocers
100–102 Shaftesbury Avenue
London, W1D 5EE
Tel: 0207 437 0014

New China Gate
18 Newport Place
London, WC1H 7PR
Tel: 0207 237 8969

New Peking Supermarket
59 Westbourne Grove
London, W2 4UA
Tel: 0207 928 8770

Newport Supermarket
28–29 Newport Court
London, WC2H 7PO
Tel: 0207 437 2386

See Woo Hong
18–20 Lisle Street
London, WC2H 7BA
Tel: 0207 439 8325

Wing Yip
395 Edgware Road
London, NW2 6LN
Tel: 0208 450 0422

Wing Yip
Oldham Road, Ancoats
Manchester, M4 5HU
Tel: 0161 832 3215

Woo Sang Supermarket
19–21 George Street, Chinatown
Manchester, M1 4HE
Tel: 0161 236 4353

Miah, A. and Co
20 Magdalen Street
Norwich, NR3 1HE
Tel: 01603 615395

Hoo Hing Commercial Centre
Freshwater Road
Chadwell Heath
Romford, RM8 1RX
Tel: 0208 548 3636
Website: www.hoohing.com

Wah-Yu Chinese Supermarket
145 High St
Swansea, SA1 1NE
Tel: 01792 650888

Hong Cheong
115 Oxford St
Swansea, SA1 3JJ
Tel: 01792 468411

Fox's Spices (mail order)
Mason's Road
Stratford-upon-Avon, CV37 9NF
Tel: 01789 266420

AUSTRALIA
Duc Hung Long Asian Store
95 The Crescent
Fairfield, NSW 2165
Tel: (02) 9728 1092

Foodtown Thai Kee Supermarket
393–399 Sussex Street
Sydney, NSW 2000
Tel: (02) 9281 2202

Harris Farm Markets
Sydney Markets
Flemongton, NSW 2140
Tel: (02) 9746 2055

Asian Supermarkets Pty Ltd
116 Charters Towers Road
Townsville, QLD 4810
Tel: (07) 4772 3997

Burlington Supermarkets
Chinatown Mall
Fortitude Valley, QLD 4006
Tel: (07) 3216 1828

The Spice and Herb Asian Shop
200 Old Cleveland Road
Capalaba, QLD 4157
Tel: (07) 3245 5300

Western Australia Kongs
 Trading Pty Ltd
8 Kingscote Street
Kewdale, WA 6105
Tel: (08) 9353 3380

NEW ZEALAND
Golden Gate Supermarket &
 Wholesalers Ltd.
8–12 Teed Street, Newmarket
Auckland Tel: (09) 523 3373

Happy Super Market
660 Dominion Road,
Mt Roskill
Auckland Tel: (09) 623 8220

Lim Garden Supermarket Centre
3 Edsel Street, Henderson
Auckland Tel: (09) 835 2599

CANADA
Arirang Oriental Food Store
1324 10 Ave Sw # 30
Calgary, AB, T3C 0J2
Tel: (403) 228 0980

T & T Supermarket
222 Cherry Street
Toronto, ON, M5A 3L2
Tel: (416) 463 8113
Website: www.tnt-supermarket.com
(16 stores across the country)

Marché Hawai
1999 Marcel Laurin, Saint-Laurent
Montreal, QC
Tel: (514) 856 0226

Hing Shing Market
1757 Kingsway, Vancouver, BC
Tel: (604) 873 4938

Star Asian Food Centre
2053 41st Avenue
W Vancouver, BC
Tel: (604) 263 2892

Tin Cheung Market
6414 Victoria Drive
Vancouver, BC
Tel: (604) 322 9237

Western Oriental Market
101–1050 Kingsway
Vancouver, BC
Tel: (604) 876 4711

Wing Sang Meat & Vegetable Market
3755 Main Street
Vancouver, BC
Tel: (604) 879 6866

Index

Publisher's acknowledgements
The publisher would like to thank
the following for permission to
reproduce their images (t = top,
b = bottom, l = left, r = right, c =
centre): 7tl Aflo Co. Ltd./Alamy; 7tr
CharlineX China Collection/Alamy;
8 Keren Su/China Span/Alamy; 9t
Mary Evans Picture Library/Alamy;
9b Sergiu Turcanu/Alamy; 10l TAO
Images Limited/Alamy; 10r Dennis
Cox/Alamy; 11tl and 11tr JTB
Photo Communications, Inc./
Alamy; 11b Keren Su/China Span/
Alamy; 12bl Keren Su/Corbis;
12br Xu Yu/Xinhua Press/Corbis;
13tl Chen Li/Xinhua Press/Corbis;
13tr CS Owsley/Demotix/Corbis;
15c iStockphoto.